BY THE SAME AUTHOR

AMERICAN WRITERS AND COMPILERS OF SACRED MUSIC

STORIES OF HYMN TUNES

BY

FRANK J. METCALF

THE ABINGDON PRESS

NEW YORK   CINCINNATI   CHICAGO

TO MY WIFE

WHO HAS SHARED MANY AN HOUR
IN RESEARCH WITH ME

PREFACE

HYMNS move man through the intellect, music makes its appeal through the emotions with that indescribable power which in the one case brings peace and rest, while in others it stirs to action. "Day is dying in the west" produces a sense of repose after the work of the day, while "Ariel," set to the hymn of Samuel Medley, "O could I speak the matchless worth," arouses the soul to expressions of praise. The national hymns of Austria, Russia, and America, as well as the "National Hymn" of George W. Warren, are inspiring to patriotism. Between these extremes are the more quiet tunes suggestive of devotion and worship.

Most of the tunes in this collection are found in one or more of the seven books that have been used as the basis of this study.

The American Hymnal, W. J. Dawson...1913
The Baptist New Praise Book........1914
The Pilgrim Hymnal (Congregational)..1904
The New Hymnal (Episcopal)..........1916
The Methodist Hymnal................1905
The Unitarian Hymnal................1914
The University Hymnal...............1907

The choice of tunes has not been an easy one. Your favorite may not be included. In one book, *The Methodist Hymnal*, there are 555 tunes. When the first choice of 101 tunes had been made for this volume, it was found that some which could hardly

7

be omitted had not been included, so these were added and others had to give place. The book as now before you contains fifty-four tunes by American composers, thirty-four by English composers, and thirteen by composers of other countries. The popularity of English writers seems to be gaining over the American. Lowell Mason and Thomas Hastings are still the leaders of American composers, but as compared with the two most popular of the English writers we find in the seven books already named a total of 297 settings of tunes by John B. Dykes, 201 by Sir Joseph Barnby, 139 by Lowell Mason, and 22 by Thomas Hastings. It may be necessary to explain that if a single tune is used four times in one book with as many different hymns it is counted as four.

Among the sources of information may be mentioned first (for English tunes) the historical edition of *Hymns Ancient and Modern,* which gives the history of all the hymns and tunes that have appeared in the four editions of that popular hymn book. *The Music of the Church Hymnary,* issued in 1901 by William Cowan and James Love, contains the history of the tunes that appeared in *The Church Hymnary,* edited by Sir John Stainer, in 1872. The earlier work of James Love, *Scottish Church Music,* has been helpful, and James T. Lightwood's *Hymn Tunes and Their Story* has been used. For tunes of American origin the only book that deals with any number of tunes is Hezekiah Butterworth's *Story of the Tunes.* Some information has been obtained from the tunes referred to by Doctor Benson in his two series of *Studies in Familiar Hymns.* Recourse has also been had to articles in various magazines, to the printed biographies of the composers, and to the stories of the tunes that have appeared at various times in the papers of the day. The biographical index of the composers of the tunes in *The Methodist Hymnal*, inserted in the *Hymns and Hymn Writers of the Church*, by Doctors Nutter and Tillett, 1911, has been consulted frequently.

FRANK J. METCALF.

Washington, D. C.

ADESTE FIDELES

UNKNOWN

"Adeste Fideles" is called "Oporto" in the Hallowell Collection, 1817, and "Portuguese Hymn" in many books. The history of this tune is interesting, but its origin is baffling. The earliest form of it in manuscript is dated 1751, and a copy is preserved in Stoneyhurst College, near Blackburn, England. This was the work of John Francis Wade, a Catholic priest, who seems to have occupied part of his time in copying music for the use of wealthy families. Two stories have been recorded to account for the origin of the tune. One assigns it to a certain Marcas Portugal, but as that personage was born in 1763, his claim to a tune in a manuscript of 1751 is impossible. The other relates to a John Reading. In the life of her father, Vincent Novello, Mrs. Clarke makes the following definite statement:

The "Adeste Fideles," although a composition of an Englishman named John Reading, obtained the name of Portuguese Hymn from its having been heard by the Duke of Leeds at the Portuguese Chapel, who imagined it to be peculiar to the service in Portugal. Being the Director of the Ancient Concerts, his Grace introduced the melody there, and it speedily became popular under the title he had given it.

There were two John Readings who were English musicians. Dr. W. H. Cummings, who investigated

11

this tune quite thoroughly, came to the conclusion that the older one, who was at one time an organist in the Winchester Cathedral, may have been the author of "Adeste Fideles." The rhythm and style of the melody alike suggest its English origin, and for lack of further proof there seems to be no reason why it should not be styled an "Old English Air."

ALETTA

WILLIAM B. BRADBURY

"Aletta" appeared in the *Jubilee*, 1857, with a mark indicating that it was a new tune, and it was set to a hymn beginning, "Weary sinner, keep thine eyes." In several other books compiled by Bradbury the hymn used is "Weary soul, no longer mourn," and this hymn, by Augustus M. Toplady, is used in one of the settings in the *Baptist Hymnal* of Doane and Johnson, 1883. Compilers have not settled upon any one hymn to be used exclusively with this tune. With seven settings in three different books there is no one that is used twice. This tune is not found in *The American Hymnal*, the *Episcopal*, the *Presbyterian*, or the *Unitarian*.

William Bachelder Bradbury was the third child in his father's family. He was born in York, Maine, of musical parentage, received part of his musical education in the school of Lowell Mason in Boston, Massachusetts, but began teaching in his native State at Machias. He later moved to New York City, where he established himself in the practice of his profession as an organist and a teacher of music. Later in life he formed a partnership with his brother and began the manufacture of pianos, which won a wide and enviable reputation. He compiled his first book, *The Young Choir*, in 1841, and during the twenty-five years following, his name is to be found

on the title pages of an average of more than two
books per year.   After his retirement from active
business he lived at Montclair, New Jersey, where he
died January 7, 1868.

AMERICA

6, 4.

HENRY CAREY

One would not expect to find the tune "America" set to any other hymn than Samuel F. Smith's "My country, 'tis of thee," in books published since 1832. In one book it is called National Hymn. It would serve no useful end to repeat the evidence which might show that strains of the tune were taken from a composition of Dr. John Bull, though it is only natural to connect his name with the English national hymn. The fact is pretty well established, however, that in 1740, at a dinner given to celebrate the taking of Portobello by the English, Henry Carey sang as his own composition the words of "God save the king," to this melody, and this assertion has never been disproved. Another most interesting fact is that its first use as a hymn tune was probably in an American book—James Lyon's *Urania*, 1761—where it is called Whitefield's Tune, and is set to the words of the anonymous hymn, "Come, thou almighty king." It is a very popular tune in England, and its earliest known form is found in the *Harmonia Anglicana*, about 1742.

Henry Carey was both a poet and a musician. Born about 1692, he was largely self-educated, became a teacher of music and spent much of his time writing for the theaters. He is remembered now by his well-known ballad "Sally in our alley," and the melody of the English national hymn, "God save the king," which is also considered as the proper tune for the American national hymn, thus happily binding together in song the two great branches of the English-speaking people.   Carey died in London, October 4, 1743.

AMSTERDAM

7, 6.

JAMES NARES

This is one of the old tunes that has been in common use for nearly two hundred years. It is usually assigned to Dr. James Nares, though sometimes called a German choral, as it is found in many German tune books. The earliest known copy of it is in *A Collection of Tunes as they are commonly sung at the Foundry*, London, 1742, often referred to as the *Foundry Collection*. It is now universally used with the hymn of Robert Seagrave, "Rise, my soul, and stretch thy wings." This hymn was first published in his collection of *Hymns for Christian Worship*, 1742, the same year that the Foundry Collection was issued, and hymn and tune, thus wedded, have remained associated to this day. Wherever the tune is introduced, there it is set with this inspiring hymn.

James Nares, son of George Nares, was born at Stanwell, in the county of Middlesex, England. The record in the parish register shows that he was baptized April 19, 1715. He was chorister in the Chapel Royal successively under Doctor Croft and Bernard Gates, and was afterward a pupil of Doctor Pepusch. He was organist in York Cathedral, 1734, and in the Chapel Royal, 1756. In the latter year he received from Cambridge the degree of Musical Doctor, and in 1757 he became Master of the Children in the place of his former teacher, Gates, a position which he held till 1780. He died in London, February 10, 1783, and was buried in Saint Margaret's, Westminster. He wrote much music for instruction and for the services of the church, both anthems and tunes.

ANGEL VOICES

8, 5, 8, 5, 8, 4, 3.

ARTHUR SEYMOUR SULLIVAN

"Angel Voices" was written in 1871 or 1872, and was introduced into *The Methodist Hymnal* of 1905 set to the hymn "Angel Voices ever singing." In a review of his *Church Hymns*, which appeared in 1874, the following remarks are found, referring to this tune: "Some of the tunes are decidedly in the weak and sentimental vein of the age, as 'Angel Voices,' which is not only feeble and dubious in its harmonic progressions (witness the consecutive octaves in the last part), but being written in 6/8 time is much too frivolous for the department of Choral Festival Hymns to which it is assigned." In the *Episcopal Hymnal*, compiled by J. Ireland Tucker, in 1894, this tune is found in the index under the name "Diapason." Such criticism does not apply to many of the tunes of Sullivan which are used in present-day books.

Arthur Seymour Sullivan was born in London, May 13, 1842. His father, Thomas, was a musician. The boy became chorister in the Chapel Royal under the famous Helmore from 1854 to 1857, and after three years of study in Leipzig (1858–1861) he was chosen organist at the church of Saint Michael's in Chester Square, where he continued from 1861 till 1867. He was a prolific composer, and one of the most popular in Britain. His best-known secular works are the operettas "Pinafore" and "The

Mikado." A large number of his church tunes appeared in *Church Hymns*, a book which he edited in 1874. The degree of Musical Doctor was given him by Cambridge University in 1876, and by Oxford in 1879, and he was knighted May 15, 1883. His death occurred in London, November 22, 1900.

ANGELS' STORY

7, 6, D.

ARTHUR HENRY MANN

The name of this tune is taken from the first lines of the hymn by Emily Huntington Miller,

> "I love to hear the story
> Which angel voices tell."

The tune was written to be used with this hymn, and first appeared in the English *Methodist Sunday School Tune Book*, 1881. It is called "Supplication," and set to this same hymn, in the *Hymnal for Schools*, by Ives and Woodman, 1895, and "Watermouth" in the *New Hymnal for the Episcopal Church*, 1916. Several recent books, as *The American Hymnal* and *The Methodist Hymnal*, use it with the hymn, "O Jesus, I have promised," which was written in 1868 by John E. Bode on the occasion of the confirmation of his two sons and a daughter.

Arthur H. Mann was born in Norwich, England, May 16, 1850. He was chorister at Norwich Cathedral under Dr. Zachariah Buck, has served as organist in a number of churches, and since 1876 has been organist and choir director at King's College, Cambridge. One of his tunes he has called "King's College." He graduated from Oxford in 1874 with the degree of Musical Bachelor and in 1882 received that of Musical Doctor. He is an honorary member of the Royal Association of Musicians, has made an especial study of and is an acknowledged authority

21

on the music of Handel, as well as other composers of
that time. He and Ebenezer Prout discovered at the
Foundling Hospital in 1894 the original wind parts
of the Messiah, and the oratorio was performed in
that year with the reconstructed score at King's
College. He edited the famous motet of Tallis,
which had been written for forty voices, and in 1895
edited the Church of England *Hymnal*.

ARIEL

C. P. M.

LOWELL MASON

The earliest appearance of the tune "Ariel" that I have found is in the Boston Academy Collection, 1836, where it is under the name of Lowell Mason, with this note: "This tune is taken from *Occasional Psalm and Hymn Tunes* by permission of the proprietors of that work." It is there set to the hymn of Samuel Medley, "O could I speak the matchless worth," and I have not found it used with any other hymn in the several books that I have examined. In some books it is said to have been arranged from Mozart by Lowell Mason in 1836. From his two trips to Europe Mr. Mason had acquired a mass of Continental music which he adapted to the use of his several collections. Among those which were arranged from this music are the tunes called "Dennis," "Naomi," and "Olmutz." In 1832 Mr. Mason organized the Boston Academy of Music, and was associated with George James Webb in its various activities. They began with the free instruction of children, and after persistent efforts proved to the school authorities in Boston that music could be taught to young children, and a period of instruction, without cost to the city, was followed by the permanent introduction of that subject into the schools of that city. Other activities of the Academy were the conducting of conventions for the teaching of music, the organization of a chorus and orchestra for the presentation of concerts, and the arranging of lectures on musical topics.   Lowell Mason has been called the father of American church music, for the reason that his methods of teaching brought the subject to the attention of the people at large, and the extensive sale of his instruction and tune books left them in the possession of the music which they had learned in his conventions.

ARLINGTON

C. M.

Thomas Augustine Arne

The overture in Arne's opera "Artaxerxes," produced at Covent Garden in 1762, contains a minuet from which the tune "Arlington" has been arranged. It was first used as a hymn tune by Ralph Harrison in his *Sacred Harmony*, in 1784, and in different books one or the other of these dates is given as the date of the tune.

Thomas A. Arne (1710–1778) was the principal composer of the eighteenth century. He was the son of a London upholsterer, was educated at Eton College for the law, but his dislike for that subject and his fondness for music resulted in his secretly studying the latter. He learned to play the flute and the violin, and practiced on a muffled spinet, so that his father would not hear him. When found out, a scene ensued, but the father became reconciled to his ambition. Arne taught his sister to develop her voice, so that she became a noted singer, and is known as the wife of Theophilus Cibber. For eighteen years Thomas was employed at Drury Lane, most of the time as leader of the band, then he transferred the scene of his labors to Covent Garden. He taught music, being especially successful in developing distinct enunciation in his pupils. He wrote music for the presentation on the stage of Milton's "Comus," and in 1740 produced the music for Mallet's "Alfred," in which his song, "Rule Britannia," appeared. This noble and characteristic melody alone would serve to place Arne among the first of song writers. His "Artaxerxes" brought him sixty guineas for its copyright, was successful from the first, and held its place on the stage for upward of three quarters of a century.

AURELIA

7. 6.

"Aurelia" was composed for the hymn "Jerusalem, the golden," whence its name "Golden," and
first appeared in *A Selection of Psalms and Hymns
arranged for the public service of the Church of
England*, edited by the Rev. Charles Kemble, the
music selected, arranged, and partly composed by
Samuel S. Wesley, 1864. It is now almost universally associated with the hymn of Samuel J.
Stone, "The Church's one foundation." It was set
to this hymn for the first time in the *Appendix to the
English Hymns Ancient and Modern*, 1868. It came
into prominence in 1872, when it was chosen to be
sung at the thanksgiving service at Saint Paul's for
the recovery of the Prince of Wales, to words especially written by Rev. Samuel J. Stone. Quite appropriate then that the tune should now be so constantly used with other words of the same writer.
Another tune by Wesley bears his middle name,
"Sebastian."

Samuel Sebastian Wesley (1810–1876) came of a
musical line. His father, Samuel, was for many
years a leading musician in London, and his grandfather was the hymn writer, Charles Wesley. He
was one of the children of the Chapel Royal, and
later organist at the Hereford and Exeter Cathedrals, the Leeds Parish Church, Winchester and
Gloucester Cathedrals. *The European Psalmist*,

27

compiled by him, was published in 1872. This work had been in preparation for at least twenty-one years, but it was not a success, and is now rarely heard of even in England. Still he was one of the greatest writers of church music, which included anthems and music for the organ.

AUSTRIA

8. 7. D.

Francis J. Haydn

The "Austrian Hymn" is found also under the names of "Austria," "Haydn," "Vienna," and "Cheadle." The melody was composed by Francis Joseph Haydn for the national hymn written by Hauschka, and was first performed on the emperor's birthday, February 12, 1797. Some idea of the original hymn may be obtained from a translation in common meter with which it was first used in England.

> "God preserve the Emp'ror Francis,
>   Sov'reign ever good and great;
> Save him, save him from mischances
>   In prosperity and state."

It came into use as a hymn-tune in 1805 in Doctor Miller's collection of Doctor Watts' *Psalms and Hymns Set to New Music;* but this adaptation was not very successful, and other attempts were made to fit it for church use, which finally resulted in the tune as now found. The most common setting for it is the hymn of John Newton, "Glorious things of thee are spoken." The story is told of William Gardiner, who issued two volumes of *Sacred Melodies* in 1812, and was a stocking manufacturer in Leicester, that he once presented Haydn with a pair of stockings on which were worked the opening bars of the "Emperor's Hymn." This melody was also used by the composer as the subject of one of the movements in his string quartet No. 77.

Haydn (1732–1809) is known as a writer of hymn-tunes chiefly from this adaptation of his "Emperor's Hymn," but he had also written other tunes for Tattershall's *Improved Psalmody*, 1794.   He is better known for his orchestral music, including symphonies, concertos, sonatas, and for the oratorio of "The Creation."

AVISON

11, 12.

Charles Avison

"Avison" is named for its composer, and was a chorus to a longer composition set to Moore's poem, "Sound the loud timbrel o'er Egypt's dark sea." It is found in a number of recent hymn books set to the hymn of William A. Muhlenberg, "Shout the glad tidings, exultingly sing." This hymn was written especially for this tune at the direct request of Bishop Hobart, and so they are fittingly used together in American hymnals. The hymn first appeared in *Hymns of the Protestant Church*, 1826.

Charles Avison was born at New Castle-upon-Tyne in 1710, spent the greater part of his life in that town, and died there May 10, 1770. He visited Italy for the study of music, and on his return to England was a pupil of Geminani. In 1736 he became organist in the church of Saint Nicholas in his native town, and occupied this position until his death, when he was succeeded by his son, and then by his grandson. He composed considerable instrumental music, such as concertos and sonatas, and was the leader of a small group of amateur musicians in the north of England. He assisted John Garth in 1757 in editing an edition of *A Paraphrase of the First Fifty Psalms*, set to music by an Italian composer, Benedetto Marcello, and printed in Venice in 1724, which was reprinted in London with English words in 1757. His "Essay on Musical Expression," 1752, was strongly and successfully assailed by William Hayes, Professor of Music at Oxford University. He pointed out many errors against the rules of composition. Shortly afterward Avison reprinted his "Essay" with a reply to the remarks of Hayes, in which he was assisted by the learned Doctor Jortin.

AVON

C. M.

Hugh Wilson

This tune was first called "Fenwick," from the name of the town where its composer was born. He had written it in common time, and it had been issued on sheets with the air and bass only. It was twenty-five years before it was used in a hymn book. It then appeared in *The Seraph;* A Selection of Psalm and Hymn Tunes, compiled by John Robertson and published in 1827 in England. It is found in many of the books now in common use as "Martyrdom," and changed to triple time. *The Methodist Hymnal* presents it under the name "Avon"; the *New Baptist Praise Book* as "Martyrdom (Avon)."

For a long time the authorship remained unknown, and it is largely due to the researches of James Love that its story was made public in his *Scottish Church Music*. From him we glean that Hugh Wilson was born in 1764, baptized December 2, and was a native of Fenwick, Ayrshire. He received his education in the village school, and was taught the shoemaking trade by his father, John Wilson. His spare moments, however, were devoted to the study of mathematics and music. He also made sundials, and set up one in the town of Fenwick which was in use for years. He occasionally led the music in the village church, and added to his income by teaching music and the ordinary branches of education.

About 1800 Wilson removed to Pollokshaws, where he made the acquaintance of William Dunn, in whose mills at Duntocher he afterward held an important situation for several years. While there he helped found the first Sunday school in that village. He died August 14, 1824. Hugh Wilson composed many other tunes, but "Avon" is the only one in present use; in fact, just before his death he caused his manuscripts containing poems, hymns, and tunes to be destroyed.

AZMON

C. M.

CARL G. GLASER

"Azmon" is one of the tunes introduced into use in this country from German sources by Lowell Mason. It is found as early as 1839 in his *Modern Psalmody*. In *The Methodist Hymnal* it has been used since 1867, and in the 1905 edition it is set to the first hymn, "O for a thousand tongues to sing," a hymn of Charles Wesley, which has stood first in the books of that denomination for over one hundred years. In Charles S. Robinson's *Songs for the Sanctuary*, 1879, it is called "Denfield." When Thomas Hastings, who was so closely associated with Lowell Mason in the compilation of music books, wished to use this melody in his *Selah*, 1856, he changed the rhythm, and beginning with a quarter note on the third count made each bar consist of a half note and a quarter note. He called his tune "Gaston," but with the exception of two tones in the last line the melody is identical with "Azmon," though the change in time renders it hardly recognizable. It has become a favorite hymn-tune in this country, and is used in many collections of school songs in Germany.

This tune was written in 1828 by Carl G. Glaser, a native of Wessenfels, Germany, where he was born May 4, 1784. The first instructor of this composer was his father, and later he studied at the Saint Thomas School in Leipzig, under Johann Adam Hiller and August Eberhard Muller, who taught him

the pianoforte, and Campagnoli, who taught him the
violin.   In 1801 he went to Leipzig to study law, but
he was more interested in music than the law, and he
gave up jurisprudence and settled in Barman, where
he spent the remainder of his years as a teacher of
pianoforte, violin, and the voice.   He also directed
choruses, and opened a music shop in Barman, which
he carried on until his death on April 16, 1829.   His
compositions were many, including motets, school
songs, and instrumental music.

BELMONT

C. M.

WILLIAM GARDINER

This tune, "Belmont," is not to be confounded with another of the same name by Samuel Webbe. James Warrington has this to say about it:

There is no doubt this tune is an adaptation from a melody in the first volume of William Gardiner's *Sacred Melodies,* but whether the air is by Gardiner I am not prepared to say. It bears a great resemblance to a German melody of the latter part of the eighteenth century, and may have been an unconscious adaptation, but Gardiner claimed it as his own. In English tune books I do not find it earlier than 1859, but in America I find it in *Spiritual Songs for Social Worship,* 1831. This was by Mason and Hastings, and it was also in the *Psalmata,* New York, 1851, where the melody is given as a double long meter, and in the latter it is attributed to the *Sacred Melodies.*

The English book referred to, dated 1859, is called *A Church Hymn and Tune Book*, and "Belmont" appeared anonymously in it. Gardiner's *Sacred Melodies*, from which this tune is taken, was published in 1812.

William Gardiner was born in Leicester, England, March 15, 1770, and died there November 16, 1853, at the age of eighty-three. He was the son of a prosperous hosier, whose position enabled him to allow his son to follow up his extraordinary love for music. He traveled much on the Continent and was personally acquainted with most of the European music writers of his day. He claimed to be the first to introduce Beethoven's music into England.

37

In 1848 he went to Bonn, the birthplace of Beethoven, to be present at the unveiling of his statue.
Queen Victoria and Prince Albert were there also,
and Gardiner was invited to sign his name under
theirs to a parchment that was deposited in the base
of the statue.

BOYLSTON

S. M.

Lowell Mason

"Boylston" is one of the oldest of the tunes written by Lowell Mason. It is found in *The Choir*, 1832, and was named for one of the towns of his native State. The number of tunes by Lowell Mason in recent hymnals exceeds that of any other American composer, but the music of the English writers Dykes and Barnby is slowly replacing the tunes of men this side of the water.

Mr. Mason (1792–1872) was born in Medfield, Massachusetts. He led the choir in that town, but when he left home it was for a clerkship in a bank in Savannah, Georgia, where he spent fourteen years. He still continued to lead choirs, and he also served as organist in some of the churches in that Southern city. All the time he was composing music and preparing a collection of church music from other sources. On a visit to the North he succeeded in having it published by the Handel and Haydn Society of Boston in 1822, and it was so popular that it passed through eighteen editions. His compilations continued until more than forty had appeared under his name. Boston soon became his home and the base of his musical activities. He accepted the methods of Pestalozzi in his teaching, and after long efforts succeeded in introducing the instruction of music into the schools of that city. He also organized his first Musical Convention in 1834 as a means of bringing music to the people at large. These were first held in or near Boston, and the results obtained were so pleasing that demands were made for an extension of their influence until many places in the West and South were reached. His own compilations were used as textbooks, and as a consequence their sales were large.

BREAD OF LIFE

6. 4. D.

WILLIAM F. SHERWIN

The organization and development of the Chautauqua Literary and Scientific Circle for the home study of the Word and other subjects of learning was the occasion for the writing of two hymns and appropriate music therefor. In 1877 a responsive service was in preparation for this institution, and Miss Mary A. Lathbury wrote a hymn to be used in it. Later it became the study hymn of the Circle, sung or repeated by thousands of eager students as they sat down to begin the lessons that had been laid out for them:

> "Break thou the bread of life,
> Dear Lord, to me,
> As thou did'st break the bread
> By Galilee."

For the summer meetings on the shores of Lake Chautauqua in New York, leaders from many denominations were gathered to instruct and entertain the earnest people who had come together for several weeks of relaxation from their daily routine, there to listen to the lectures and enjoy the concerts and the wholesome forms of amusement. Other Assemblies were organized in various places throughout the country, and large groups of persons devoted much of their summer vacation to the benefit of their minds as well as their physical beings.

William Fiske Sherwin was a Baptist, and, as a

prominent music teacher and successful leader of choirs, he was called to Chautauqua to direct the musical features of the programs there. He it was who wrote the music to which Miss Lathbury's study hymn was sung, and the two have been introduced into many of the church hymnals, and have come into common use. He also wrote the tune for Miss Lathbury's evening hymn, "Day is dying in the west."

CAROL

C. M. D.

RICHARD S. WILLIS

Two of the Christmas hymns in common use were written by Edmund H. Sears—"It came upon the midnight clear" and "Calm on the listening ear of night." "Carol" has been adopted as a Christmas tune and is set to each of these in various books, though more frequently to the first one named. 1850 is the date assigned for its composition.

Richard Storrs Willis, born February 10, 1819, devoted much of his life to the study and promotion of music. He was a graduate of Yale in the class of 1841, and while in college wrote music for the college choir. After a period spent in the study of music in Germany, he returned to Yale to teach colloquial German to its students. It was there that he met Charles A. Dana, upon whose advice he entered the field of journalism. He first bought the *Musical Times*, which had been founded in New York about 1849 by Saroni, and which was later changed to the *Musical World*. Its value in the collection of items of musical lore is attested by John M. Moore, who states that from this periodical he obtained considerable material which could be obtained nowhere else to embody in his *Cyclopedia of Music*. In 1862 Willis established the magazine, *Once a Month*. He was also the editor of the American edition of the *Life of Mendelssohn*, 1865. He wrote three books on the subject of music: *Church Chorals and Choir*

43

Studies, 1854; *Our Church Music,* 1855; and *Carols and Music Poems,* 1860.   He also contributed a composition, both words and tune, to *National Hymns,* prepared by Richard Grant White in 1861.   He died in Detroit, Michigan, May 7, 1900, at the age of eighty-one.

CLOSE TO THEE

8. 7.

Silas J. Vail

Most of the music of Mr. Vail now in common use is of such a character that it has been slow to find its way into the denominational hymnals. Many of his tunes had a refrain, which was a bar to their introduction into the regular hymn books. He set to music many of the hymns of Fanny Crosby. His tunes are known usually only by the first line of the hymn with which they are used, such as "Scatter seeds of kindness," "The Gate ajar for me" and "Nothing but leaves." A tune written for a particular hymn is generally suggested by the words of that hymn. Mr. Vail assisted Sylvester Main in the compilation of *The Dayspring*, 1859, which contained twenty-five of his compositions, contributed to *The Methodist Hymnal*, edited by Philip Phillips, 1869; *The Baptist Praise Book*, 1872; and *The Revivalist*, 1872.

Silas Jones Vail was born in Brooklyn, October 6, 1818. He learned the hatter's trade in Danbury, Connecticut, then returned to New York, where he was employed in a hat store. Later he set up in business for himself in the same line, and was very successful. During the war period he compiled for Horace Waters *The Athenæum Collection*, a book that is now very rare, and is sought after for the reason that twenty-five or more pieces were written for it by Stephen Collins Foster. It seems very

45

strange that a book published no earlier than the Civil War should be so seldom found at the present time. When a catalogue was made in 1915 of the first editions of Foster by the Library of Congress, even that large collection did not have one, and its entries were made from a borrowed copy. Since then our national library has obtained one, and one has been added to the possessions of the present writer. Mr. Vail died May 20, 1884, in Brooklyn, New York.

CORONATION

C. M.

OLIVER HOLDEN

The words of Edward Perronet's hymn, "All hail the power of Jesus' name," are associated with two tunes. In this country the recent hymn books give a choice of both "Coronation" and "Miles Lane," but in the few English books consulted "Miles Lane" is invariably used. "Coronation" was first published in a compilation by its author, Oliver Holden, in 1793, *Union Harmony, or Universal Collection of Sacred Music*, in two volumes. In that book it is set with the hymn of "Perronet," although it is there erroneously stated that the words are "by the Rev. Mr. Medley."

Oliver Holden was a native of Shirley, Massachusetts, where he was born September 18, 1765. After the burning of Charlestown at the time of the battle of Bunker Hill, he moved to that town, where its rebuilding promised employment. He prospered in business, and also devoted much of his time to the writing of music and the compilation of music books. He became the editor of the sixth edition of the *Worcester Collection* in 1797, which had previously been published under the direction of Isaiah Thomas. More than twenty tunes were contributed by him to the different books which he compiled. The organ on which he first played his tunes, and on which "Coronation" was composed, is now in the rooms of the Bostonian Society, and some years ago the writer enjoyed the privilege of being one of a group of a dozen or more who stood around this organ on the Fourth of July and sang to its accompaniment "My country, 'tis of thee."

CRUSADERS' HYMN

5, 6, 8, 5, 5, 8.

Arranged by RICHARD S. WILLIS

It is a pretty story that "An unexpected treasure was discovered in 1850 in the guise of a Crusaders' hymn. It was found in Westphalia amid a number of other curious relics, and, according to the traditional text by which it was accompanied, used to be sung by the German pilgrims on their way to Jerusalem. It may therefore be regarded as a national air at that time. It achieved a great popularity at the time of its discovery, and has already become a chief favorite with the people. It is sung by all classes and ages, from the shepherd on the hillside to the lisping urchin in the nursery." The tune used in the hymn books of America was arranged by Richard S. Willis, and the words always used with it are a translation from a German hymn, "Fairest Lord Jesus." The history of both tune and hymn was investigated by Doctor Julian, who says that there is not the shadow of foundation for the story, for the words have not been traced to an earlier date than 1677, and the earliest form of the tune is found in a collection of Silesian folk-songs by Hoffman and Richter, 1842. In the preface of this collection it is stated that the tune was one which the hay-makers sang, and upon further acquaintance with the people many other songs were found which seemed worthy of preservation in print. The tune is known as "Ascalon" in English books, where it was first adapted as a hymn tune by Gauntlett. The melody has been changed in some books. Richard S. Willis used the translation in his *Church Chorals*, 1850, where he stated that he did not know the translator. The hymn and tune were used in the *Plymouth Collection*, 1855, and generally in hymn books since.

DARWALL

6. 8.

JOHN DARWALL

The tune "Darwall" takes its name from the composer, John Darwall. It is first found in Aaron Williams' *Psalmodist*, 1770, for the 148th psalm. Darwall wrote a tune for each of the one hundred and fifty psalms, but all of them have not been published. He made two manuscript copies of these tunes, which he dated December 10, 1783, and as late as 1905 this autograph collection was in the possession of his grandson, the Rev. Lester Darwall. This tune is to be found in the *Methodist Harmonist* of 1837, and in many books as "Darwall," but in the Presbyterian *Hymnal* it is given its original title, "Darwall's 148th."

The Rev. John Darwall was baptized January 13, 1731, at Haughton, England. He was educated at the Manchester Grammar School and at Brazenose College, Oxford, entering the latter at the age of fourteen. He was appointed curate of Saint Matthew's, Walsall, of which church he later became vicar, serving there for twenty years, and there he died in December, 1789. The story of the opening of the organ at Walsall is taken from James T. Lightwood's *Hymn Tunes and Their Story*, where it is quoted from the *Gentleman's Magazine* for 1800. In Whit week, 1773, some anthems were performed by the Walsall singers in the parish church. The organ was then opened by Doctor Alcock. On the next Sunday in the afternoon it was first played in full congregation by Mr. Balam, the church organist, who was blind. The sermon by Mr. Darwall was from the text, "Praise Him with stringed instruments and organs." After the sermon the entire 148th psalm, new version, was sung to a new tune of the vicar's composing, and the whole concluded with appropriate prayer and the blessing.

DENNIS

S. M.

JOHANN GEORG NAEGALI

When Lowell Mason visited Europe he purchased some of the manuscripts of Naegali, and on his return to this country arranged them for hymn-tunes in the books which he was constantly preparing for publication. One of these he called "Dennis," and it appeared in 1845 in *The Psaltery*, set to the hymn of Philip Doddridge, "How gentle God's commands." It has been in common use ever since that time, and is frequently used several times in a single book, set to different hymns, but the original setting as given above is sure to be with it once in every book. Although this is the only tune of this writer that is now in use in current hymn books, several others were in use years ago. The *American Tune Book*, which was planned to contain tunes which are widely popular in America, was printed in 1869; and had three tunes besides "Dennis" by Naegali; and *The Sabbath*, compiled by Charles Everest in Philadelphia, has two not included in the four just referred to.

The name of the composer is usually written in the shortened form of Hans G. Naegali. He was a Swiss musician, composer, and publisher, and was also somewhat of a poet. Born near Zurich in 1768, he established his music business in that city in 1792. From his presses there were issued many of the standard pieces, which have become classics—compositions of Beethoven, Weber, and Handel—and

they were put up in large oblong folio form with
distinctive clearness and beauty. In 1803 he started
a periodical in which he brought out new works by
Clementi, Cramer, and others. Thus his entire life
was devoted to the development of music in his native
province, and he died in Zurich, December 26, 1836.

DIX

7s

CONRAD KOCHER

The tune "Dix" is arranged from a chorale by
Conrad Kocher, and is introduced into a German
book which he edited in 1838. It was first used in
its present form in the original edition of *Hymns
Ancient and Modern*, 1861, whose editor, W. H.
Monk, had arranged it for that book. It was there
set to the words, "As with gladness men of old," by
William Chatterton Dix, whence its name. At present it is generally set to this hymn, but several other
hymns of this meter are also found with it, the one
most frequently used beginning, "For the beauty of
the earth," by Folliott S. Pierpont. The *National
Hymn Book* has the name "Dix," with an alternate
title of "Orisons."

Conrad Kocher was born in Ditzinger in Wurtem-
berg, December 16, 1786. He studied the pianoforte in Saint Petersburg, and at the age of seventeen
became a tutor there; but teaching did not find the
favor with him that music did, and under the influence of Clementi he decided to relinquish the former.
He then went to Rome, where his study of the works
of Palestrina led to the formation of a plan for the
general reform of church music in his native country. On his return he founded a church choral
society at Stuttgart, which resulted in popularizing
four-part singing in the churches. He was organist
in the "Stiftskirche" in Stuttgart from 1827 to 1865,

a period of thirty-eight years, received the degree of Ph.D. from Tübingen University in 1852, and in 1854 published a large collection of *Chorales*. He did considerable work in the revision of various hymn books, and contributed new tunes to them. He died in Stuttgart March 12, 1872, having passed his eighty-fifth birthday.

DUANE STREET

L. M. D.

The centenary sermon on "The History and Character of Methodism" was preached in 1839 in the Duane Street Methodist Church in New York by its pastor, the Rev. George Coles. This minister had been one of the editors of the *Methodist Harmonist*, and had written three tunes especially for that book: later he composed one which he called "Duane Street." This is the only one of his tunes that became popular. In the *Plymouth Hymnal*, edited by Lyman Abbott in 1893, it is called "Wanderer," and is set to the hymn of James Montgomery, "A poor wayfaring man of grief," as it is in several other books. But its more frequent setting is John Cennick's "Jesus, my all, to heaven is gone."

The composer tells us that in his youth music was his only recreation, and he became so passionately fond of it as to lose all relish for the sports and amusements of other boys. He was a native of England, emigrated to America when a young man, joined the New York Methodist Conference, and spent the remaining years of his life in the service of that church. For twelve years he was assistant editor of The Christian Advocate, and for three years editor of the Sunday School Advocate and other Sunday-school literature. He kept a diary for over fifty years, from which he wrote *My Youthful Days* and *My First Seven Years in America*. A

57

Scripture Concordance was published in 1847. He tells that a young doctor of his acquaintance was a fine flute player, and as he had a slight knowledge of that instrument, they practiced together for mutual improvement. The doctor played first flute, he second flute, and soon their employer joined them with a violoncello and the trio took up Leach's Anthems. After a while they could have accompanied a choir.

DUKE STREET

L. M.

JOHN HATTON

Very few facts have been found about John Hatton, the composer of the tune "Duke Street." He was born at Warrenton, near Liverpool, but the date of his birth has not been discovered. In his later years he resided on Duke Street in the district of Saint Helens, in the township of Windle, not far from his native town, and from these facts it is easy to see why this one of his tunes should be called by the three names, "Duke Street," "Saint Helens," and "Windle." The first name is the one most commonly used in the hymnals of the present day. John Hatton died in 1793, and his funeral sermon was preached in the Presbyterian chapel at Saint Helens on December 13. This date gives an idea of the approximate period covered by his life.

"Duke Street" has not been found in any collection of tunes issued prior to the death of its author in 1793, though the date assigned for its composition is 1790. It is first found in *A Select Collection of Psalm and Hymn Tunes*, by the late Henry Boyd, teacher of psalmody, Glasgow, 1793. It is there headed "Addison's Nineteenth Psalm," but no composer's name is attached. It is next found in a collection of tunes edited by William Dixon about 1805. The name of this book is *Euphonia*. . . . Sixty-two Psalm and Hymn Tunes in four parts, for the Congregation of All Saints Church, Liverpool.

There the tune appeared under its common name, and was attributed to Hatton. As Dixon was a music engraver, and teacher in Liverpool, it is safe to assume that he knew the facts about the writing of this tune. It is found in this country as early as 1828 in the Handel and Haydn Collection, and is used in almost every hymn book issued since that date.

EASTER HYMN

7s.

Lyra Davidica

The earliest appearance of this tune, so far as discovered, is in a book called *Lyra Davidica*, dated 1708. It is there called "The Resurrection." In some books it is given the name "Worgan," on the assumption that it was written by John Worgan. But as he was not born until after 1708, his claim to it is quickly settled. Other names have been from time to time proposed but no definite ascription can be made, as the names of the composers are not set to any of the tunes in that book. It was probably written to Charles Wesley's Easter hymn, "Christ, the Lord, is risen to-day," and was used in his *Foundry Hymn Book*, 1742. The modern form of the tune was first used in the second edition of Arnold's *Complete Psalmodist*, 1749. *Lyra Davidica* was an engraved book (F. H. sculpsit) and was *A Collection of Divine Songs and Hymns*, partly new-composed, partly translated from the High German and Latin Hymns; and set to easy and pleasant tunes, for more general use. Only a single copy of this book is known. The history of this unique book is interesting. It can be traced back only to the year 1800, when an inscription in the book informs us that it was given by a Mr. Skillern to Doctor Calcott, the famous glee composer. After Calcott's death his library was dispersed by auction, and the book became the property of William Ayrton, a well-known musical critic, and a man of considerable literary attainments. For ten years he conducted *The Harmonican,* one of the best musical journals of the early part of the last century. He died in 1858 and at the sale of his library the *Lyra* was sold for eight shillings six pence. Two years later it passed into the keeping of the British Museum, the owner receiving a guinea and a half for his treasure.

EIN' FESTE BURG

P. M.

Martin Luther

Luther's hymn is extensively popular. Julian notes eighteen different translations that are in common use in English and American hymn books, thirty-one that are not in recent books, and then adds fifteen more from American poets, making sixty-three translations of this one hymn into the English language. What other hymn can boast so many admirers? The tune he wrote for it is invariably used with it, almost necessarily on account of the peculiar meter. Both hymn and tune appeared in a German hymn book by J. Klug, printed in Wurtemburg, 1529. Julian's comment is as follows: "An effort has been recently made to show that this is a patchwork of snatches from various portions of the Roman Gradual, which Luther as a monk must have often sung. But even if this were clearly shown, to Luther would still be due the honor of smelting these scattered fragments, and producing from them a glorious melody, now all of one piece." It became the battle hymn of the Reformation, the national song of Protestant Germany, and has continued its inspiring effects down to the present time.

The two dates, 1483, 1546, will locate Luther in the history of the world. At the age of eighteen he entered the University of Erfurt for the purpose of studying law, but events changed the trend of his life, and he entered a monastery. On October 31,

1495, aroused by the sale of indulgences by Tetzel, he nailed his famous ninety-five theses to the door of the cathedral. An important piece of writing that he did was the translation of the Bible into the German language, occupying his time from 1521 to 1534.

EUCHARIST

L. M.

ISAAC B. WOODBURY

This tune is called "Olivet" in Woodbury's *New Lute of Zion*, 1856, where it is set to Isaac Watts' hymn, "When I survey the wondrous cross." Its name was changed to "Eucharist" to avoid confusing it with Lowell Mason's tune of that name, which is used with Ray Palmer's hymn, "My faith looks up to Thee."

Many of the tunes of Isaac B. Woodbury (1819–1858) have passed into common use. "Siloam" is probably the best known. "Nearer Home" is sometimes called "Woodbury," and sometimes has as a title the first line of the hymn with which it is often used, "Forever with the Lord." "Selena" and "Dornnance" are other tunes frequently met with. Of his secular compositions "Speed Away" is well known. He was assisted by Benjamin F. Baker in the preparation of *The Choral*, 1845, and *The Timbrel*, 1848, while the list of his own books, beginning with 1850, numbers at least twenty in the eight remaining years of his life. A few titles are *The Dulcimer, Cythera, New Lute of Zion, The Sacred Timbrel, The Dayspring, Harp of the South, The Thanksgiving, The Youth's Song Book, The Sunday School Singing Book* and *The Sunday School Lute*. He had planned to found a musical institution with the money he had accumulated by his strict economy, but as he left a family of six young children his funds were diverted to their care and education. Had he lived to the allotted years of man, threescore and ten, his monument might have been a different one from the simple music which he wrote, and which has found such a large audience with worshiping assemblies. He wrote with remarkable fluency, and it was surprising how much he could accomplish in a short space of time.

EVENING PRAISE

7, 4.

William F. Sherwin

"Day is dying in the west" was written by Miss Mary A. Lathbury for use in a vesper service at Chautauqua, and the music for it was composed by William F. Sherwin. The hymn had originally only two stanzas, but in more recent books into which it has been introduced there are two additional ones, and that is the version inserted in her book of collected poems. A more appropriate title for this tune, "Chautauqua," is used in several books.

William F. Sherwin was a native of Buckland, in Franklin County, Massachusetts, where he was born March 14, 1826. He was leading a chorus choir at the age of fifteen, and his success with singers led to the choice of him as director of the choruses organized at the Chautauqua Assemblies. Here he would take a group of one or two hundred people, who had never sung together, organize them into a chorus, and at the end of a week he would have them prepared to present Gaul's "Holy City," or some other piece of difficult music. Much of the writer's love for music and appreciation of its beauties was acquired under the direction of Professor Sherwin at several sessions of these Assemblies. A writer in the Independent wrote some time ago that "Sherwin was a genial tyrant of the baton, who would scold his chorus till they cried, and then heal all hearts with his 'Day is dying in the west.' " Many a time has the

67

writer attended a vesper service in the Hall on the
Hill, and as the twilight began to gather joined in
the singing of

> "Day is dying in the west.
> Heaven is touching earth with rest;
> Wait and worship while the night
> Sets her evening lamps alight
> Through all the sky."

EVENING PRAYER

8, 7.

George C. Stebbins

The music of "Evening Prayer" was written by Mr. Stebbins as a response to be used after the prayer at the morning service when he had charge of the music at Tremont Temple in Boston. Two years later, while he was assisting in evangelistic meetings in Providence, it occurred to him that if he could find a suitable hymn for it, it might serve a larger purpose. He finally settled upon James Edmeston's hymn, "Saviour, breathe an evening blessing," and thus the music written for the morning prayer came to be associated with an evening hymn. He arranged it for a male choir of two hundred voices and it became a great favorite. During the Boxer movement in China it was frequently sung by the missionaries, who realized that

> "Though destruction walk around us,
> Though the arrows past us fly,
> Angel guards from Thee surround us,
> We are safe if Thou art nigh."

George Coles Stebbins was born February 26, 1846, in Orleans County, in northern New York. When twelve years old he enjoyed the privileges of the singing school in the red brick schoolhouse, and at twenty-one he began the cultivation of his voice under a teacher in Buffalo. After his marriage he located in Chicago, where he found employment leading choirs and as a clerk in the music store of Lyon

69

and Healy. His engagement here was cut short by
the great fire in 1871. His meeting with Moody and
Sankey changed the program of his life, and for
many years thereafter he was associated with them
in their religious labors. He followed them in their
work in England, and in 1889 visited India, Egypt,
and Palestine, where his singing was a welcome inci-
dent at every stop.

EWING

7, 6, D.

ALEXANDER EWING

The tune "Ewing" was composed in the year 1853, and first printed on slips. It appeared in a book as "Saint Bebe's" in the Rev. J. Gray's *Manual of Psalm and Hymn Tunes*, 1857, in three quarter time. It was altered to common time when used in *Hymns Ancient and Modern*, 1861. The composer says, "In my opinion the alteration of the rhythm has very much vulgarized my little tune. It now seems to me a good deal like a polka. I hate to hear it." The changes were made without consulting him, as he was at that time in another quarter of the globe. It was composed for a portion, though a different portion, of the translation of John Mason Neale from a long Latin poem of Bernard, but is now generally set to "Jerusalem, the Golden." It is called "Jerusalem" in the Unitarian Hymn Book, and "Jenner" in the National Hymn Book. Doctor Neale recommends this tune when he writes, "I have so often been asked to what tune the words of Bernard may be sung, that I may here mention that of Mr. Ewing, the earliest written, the best known, and with children the most popular; no small proof in my estimation of the goodness of church music."

Alexander Ewing was an accomplished amateur musician. He was born in Aberdeen, January 3, 1830, studied law, but did not like it, then went to Germany to study the language of that country, and music. The major part of his career was in the army, which he entered in 1855, and he took part in the campaigns in the Crimea, in South Australia, and in China, retiring to civil life in 1889 as a lieutenant colonel. He married, in 1867, Miss Julia Horatia Gatty, a writer of short stories for the young. She died in 1885; her husband died July 11, 1895, at Taunton.

FEDERAL STREET

L. M.

HENRY K. OLIVER

"Federal Street" was the name of the street in Salem on which Doctor Oliver lived in his later years, and was also the street in Boston on which stood the church which he attended when a child. The tune is one of those general tunes, set to a variety of hymns. It was written in 1832 to the meter of Miss Steele's hymn, beginning, "So fades the lovely blooming flower," suggested by the ending of a story he had been reading. The tune came into the possession of Lowell Mason, who was always on the lookout for new tunes to use in his rapidly increasing number of music books, and it was printed in the Boston Academy's *Collection of Church Music* in 1836. Here it was set to the last stanza of Miss Steele's hymn, the first line of which is "See gentle Patience smile on pain." This single stanza is also the only one used with the tune as it is printed in Doctor Oliver's own *Collection of Hymn and Psalm Tunes*, published by Oliver Ditson and Company in Boston in 1860. Since that time it has been used with many hymns, the most common one being that of Joseph Grigg, "Jesus, and shall it ever be."

Henry Kemble Oliver was born in Beverly, Massachusetts, November 24, 1800, was educated in the schools of Boston, took half of his college course at Harvard, and graduated from Dartmouth college in

1818. In after years Harvard sought to reclaim him by granting him the degree of A.B. and A.M. in 1862, and placing his name among the class of 1818. In public life he served as adjutant-general of Massachusetts from 1844 to 1848; was superintendent of the Atlantic Cotton Mills in Lawrence for the next ten years, and was State treasurer during the period of the Civil War. He died August 12, 1885.

FISK

7s.

Calvin Sears Harrington

Wesleyan University, Middletown, Connecticut, has furnished a number of names to American psalmody. One of the earliest was Calvin Sears Harrington, of the class of 1852, born May 17, 1826, in Saint Johnsbury, Vermont. His entire life was devoted to educational work, during the last twenty-five years of which he was professor of Greek at his Alma Mater. He was one of the committee whose work in the revision of *The Methodist Hymnal* appeared in 1878. In the *Hymnal* of 1905 he has a tune called "Fisk," one of the honored names of his denomination. He wrote the tune to which is sung the hymn beginning, "In some way or other the Lord will provide." In *Many Voices*, 1891, this tune is given the name of "Harrington." He also wrote the tune usually called "Homeward Bound," set to the hymn, "Out on an ocean all boundless we ride," which for a time was among the long list of the anonymous, but which is now known to have been written (one book gives the date as 1853) by the first president of Boston University, and now (1927) president emeritus, William Fairfield Warren. Doctor Harrington died in 1886 at Middletown.

His son, Karl Pomeroy Harrington, of the class of 1882, has been professor of the Latin language at Wesleyan since 1905. He has served as organist and music director in a number of churches in places where he has happened to be located in his profession of teaching. He was musical editor of *The Methodist Hymnal* of 1905, and furnished for that book five of its tunes, one of which is the beautiful "Christmas Song," one of the three tunes set to the hymn of Josiah G. Holland, "There's a song in the air."

FOUNDATION

11s.

UNKNOWN

The history of this tune, and its ascription to Anne Steele, furnishes a real illustration of the fact that when once a misstatement has started it is very difficult to overtake it and correct it. Following the usage of the tune backward from quite recent books we find it in Rodeheaver's *Gospel Songs*, 1922; in *Triumphant Songs*, 1894; and the *Otterbein Hymnal*, 1890. In the last named book we are getting near to the truth when we find after the name "Foundation" an explanatory phrase, "an American Spiritual." There can be little doubt but that the melody of the tune had its origin among the people to whom are ascribed the "Negro Spirituals." The tune is found in *The Methodist Hymnal*, 1905, set to "How firm a foundation," whence the name.

But now the question arises, How comes it that it should be ascribed to Anne Steele as its composer? The only person of that name known to hymnologists was a writer of religious verse, and many of her pieces have been introduced into the hymn books of various denominations. We cannot believe that she ever composed a tune, at least for print. The hymnal of the Methodist Episcopal Church, South, c. 1889, furnishes the probable solution of the problem. Here the tune "Foundation" is set on the lower half of the page, following a

77

hymn by Anne Steele, and her name, on account of the crowding on that page, comes so near the place over the tune where the name of the composer usually stands that someone, who borrowed the tune from this book, wrongfully took also the name of the writer of the upper hymn for the composer of the tune below, and the error has been copied from book to book without question as to the real fact.

GERMANY
L. M.

Ludwig van Beethoven

In 1815 William Gardner published the tune "Germany" in the second volume of his *Sacred Melodies* from Haydn, Mozart, and Beethoven, adapted to the best English poets, and wrote "subject from Beethoven." In some books it is "ascribed to Beethoven," in others "arranged from Beethoven," and in the *Handel and Haydn Collection of Sacred Music*, compiled by Lowell Mason, it bears the name "Beethoven," without further expression as to origin. The *University Hymn Book*, 1896, states that, although usually attributed to him, Sir George Grove and other authorities are of the opinion that it is not from any of his works. It is much easier to prove a positive statement than a negative one, and the fact that the earlier writers who lived during the lifetime of this great musician found evidence that it was of his composition should have considerable weight against the investigators of later times. It does not appear to have been wedded to any particular hymn, though in the Methodist and Presbyterian books of recent date it is set to that of Doctor Frank Mason North, "Where cross the crowded ways of life."

Ludwig van Beethoven was born at Bonn, on the Rhine, December 16, 1772. His grandfather was a bass singer, his father a tenor. He was instructed by the court organists at Bonn, studied later under Haydn at Vienna, and on his return was for a while

79

assistant organist at Bonn. He then went to Vienna, which was at that period the musical center of Europe, where he spent most of the balance of his life, and he died there March 26, 1827.

GREENVILLE

8, 7, 61

JEAN JACQUES ROUSSEAU

The melody of "Greenville" is taken from the opera "Le Devin du Village" ("The Soothsayer of the Village"), which was first produced before the king of France at Fontainebleau on October 18, 1752. The words and music in the opera were both original with Rousseau. For seventy-five years this opera was constantly presented on the stage, but since that time its use has been infrequent. The earliest appearance as a hymn tune seems to be in the second edition of the *Handel and Haydn Collection of Church Music*, printed in 1823, where it is called "Greenville." In England it is found in Cotterill's *Christian Psalmody*, 1831, under the name "Communion." In *Sacred Melodies*, 1843, it is called "Rousseau," and in some other books it is called "Rousseau's Dream." It is said that this French composer fell asleep one day, and dreamed that he was taken to heaven, where he saw the angels of God standing about the throne, and heard them singing this tune. As soon as he awoke he wrote it down, therefore it should properly be called "Rousseau's Dream."

Jean Jacques Rousseau was born June 28, 1712, in Geneva, of French parentage, whose ancestors had lived in that city for more than one hundred years prior to his birth. He was educated as a Protestant, but in later years became a deist. He had little instruction in music, being mostly self taught, yet he wrote five operas, besides a number of essays and papers on music. While in Geneva he met Diderot, who was compiling an "Encyclopédie," and he furnished the musical articles for it. These articles, with others on the same subject, were gathered into a volume in 1767 as a *Dictionary of Music,* which was translated into English in 1771. He died near Paris, July 2, 1778.

GROSTETTE

L. M.

HENRY W. GREATOREX

Perhaps the "Gloria Patri" of Greatorex is better known than any of his hymn-tunes, and yet it is only a few years since many of the latter were in common use. "Leighton," "Geer," and "Bemerton," as well as "Grostette," are still to be found in many books.

Henry Wellington Greatorex was born in England in 1813, came to America and began his labors as an organist in Hartford, Connecticut. He later moved to New York City, where he held similar positions and from whence he went to South Carolina, where his life was cut short by the epidemic of yellow fever in 1858. In 1851 he published a *Collection of Sacred Music*. Many impressions of this book were made, and while the ownership of the copyright remained in the name of Greatorex, or his widow, the printing changed hands from A. C. Goodman, of Hartford, to the John Church Publishing Company, New York, and finally passed into the control of the Oliver Ditson Company, of Boston. This collection has thirty-seven pieces marked H. W. G., including the four mentioned above, besides seventeen chants and other pieces. The music was printed on four staves, but the alto and tenor were also written in smaller notes on the two lower lines, so that the organist had only two staves to follow instead of four. He recommended that, for the promotion of congregational singing, the same words be used to the same tunes invariably, so that the two will become associated, and thus help the people in their singing. The time marks are also omitted from the music, leaving the musician to determine the time from the divisions by the bars.

GUIDE

7s. D.

MARCUS M. WELLS

Mr. Hubert P. Main has given the history of this tune, and many of the facts stated by him are repeated here. It was sent in October, 1858, to the office of the New York Musical Pioneer, when the editor of that paper, Isaac B. Woodbury, was on a trip south for his health. It therefore fell to Mr. Main to select the material for the November issue, in which both words and tune first appeared. It was printed in *The Psalm King*, 1866, in *Winnowed Hymns*, 1873, and in *Gospel Hymns and Sacred Songs*, 1875, the last two of which were published by the Biglow and Main Company. No specific name was given to it, but it was printed with the first line of the hymn as its heading. In several books it is called "Faithful Guide," while in others its title is shortened to the one word, "Guide." It is called "Pelton" in *The Dayspring*, 1859; "Eucharist" in *Many Voices*, 1891, edited by T. DeWitt Talmage; and "Taylor" as a sub-title in *In Excelsis*, 1905.

The author of both tune and the words usually set to it was Marcus Morris Wells, born in Otsego, New York, October 2, 1815. His version of its composition is as follows: "On a Saturday afternoon in October, 1858, while at work in my corn field, the sentiment of the hymn 'Holy Spirit, Faithful Guide,' came to me. The next day, Sunday, being a very stormy day, I finished the hymn and wrote a tune for

85

it." In early manhood he went to Buffalo, where he was converted in a mission Baptist church. Later he settled in Hartwick, where he spent the remainder of his life, occupied in farming and the making of farm implements. He died July 17, 1895, and a memorial window was inscribed to his memory in the Baptist church of that town.

HANKEY

7. 6. D.

William G. Fischer

"Hankey" is most appropriately named, as it was written for and is always found with the hymn of Catherine Hankey. This name has come into use only quite recently, the first line of the hymn having been used over the earlier appearances of the tune. The verses of the hymn are part of a long poem reciting the life of Christ, and were not intended for a hymn. Certain ones of them were taken, and Mr. Fischer wrote music for them, but the result did not satisfy him, as it seemed incomplete. One night, after he had retired, the refrain came into his head. This gave it a finished ending, and made it more suitable for a gospel song.

William Gustavus Fischer was born in Baltimore, October 14, 1835. He began his musical work in church while he was yet a boy. For the ten years from 1858 to 1868 he was a teacher of music in Girard College, and then entered the music trade in Philadelphia, where he was a pioneer in the piano business. During the Moody and Sankey campaign, which was held in his home city, he was the leader of the chorus of one thousand voices, and during the bicentennial of the landing of William Penn he also conducted a large chorus of Welsh singers. Many of his tunes are in common use, such as those set to the hymns, "Whiter than snow," "I am trusting, Lord, in thee," "A little talk with Jesus" and "O sometimes the shadows are deep." A short time before his death, which occurred in Philadelphia, August 12, 1912, he was present at an international Sunday School Convention presided over by John Wanamaker and was called to the platform to be presented to the vast gathering, while they were singing his famous music, set to the hymn, "I love to tell the story."

HANOVER

10, 11

William Croft

This tune is first found in the sixth edition of the *Supplement* to the New Version of the Psalms, 1708, by John Playford. It is there called "A new tune for the 149th Psalm of the New Version and the 104th Psalm of the Old." The notes are diamond shaped, and the melody is somewhat different from that found in present use. It was first called "Hanover" in Gawthorne's *Harmonia Perfecta*, 1731. In 1762 William Riley issued his *Parochial Psalmody*, and this has "Hanover" in a version very nearly like that now used. It has appeared under a number of names. It is "Bromswick" in the *Foundry Tune Book* of 1742, and is sometimes found as "Tally's," under the supposition that it was by Tallis. In the collection of tunes called the *People's Music Book*, edited by J. Turle and E. Taylor, it is called "Old 104th" and has Handel's name attached to it; but in the index it is credited to Doctor Croft, and the following note is added: "This tune has been ascertained to be the composition of Doctor Croft, by satisfactory evidence, since the page in which it is contained was printed." As the tune appeared in many collections which were published during the period of Handel's residence in England, and in none of them is he named as composer, his claim is quickly disposed of.

William Croft was one of the first of Britain's

church composers. He was born at Nether-Eating-ton, six miles from Stratford, in 1678, and was bap-tized December 30 of that year. He studied under the famous John Blow, received the degree of Musical Doctor from Oxford in 1713, and became organist of Westminster Abbey in 1708. Upon his death at Bath, August 14, 1727, he was accorded a burial place in Westminster Abbey.

HOLLEY

GEORGE HEWS

"Holley" seems to have been the most popular of the tunes of George Hews, for it is the only one now found in recent books. He wrote many tunes, and in the Baptist *Service of Song*, 1871, the editors express their acknowledgments for the free use they had been given of his valuable manuscript music, and for the number of selections they had made from it. "Holley" first appeared in the Boston Academy's *Collection of Church Music*, 1835, and was there set to the hymn, "Softly now the light of day," written by George Washington Doane in 1824.

George Hews was born in Weston, Massachusetts, January 6, 1806, and died in Boston, July 4, 1873. He joined the Handel and Haydn Society in 1830, served as its vice-president from 1854 to 1858, and held many other less prominent positions in its government. He was one of the oldest manufacturers of pianos, having established his business as early as 1840, and a number of patents were awarded to him for improvements, one of which was styled "Hews Patent American Action." From 1848 to 1851 the meetings of the Harvard Musical Association, of which he was made an honorary member, were held in his rooms in Boston. For many years he was organist in the Brattle Street Church in Boston, and he was intimately associated with the musical interests in that city. Besides his tunes his compositions included much instrumental music, such as marches, waltzes and quicksteps, and he also wrote many pieces of both secular and sacred vocal music, which made his name generally known among the musical people of his day.

HUMMEL
C. M.
CHARLES ZEUNER

"Hummel" first appeared in the *American Harp*, a music book of the oblong type, printed in 1832, where it is set to the hymn of Isaac Watts, "Awake, ye saints, to praise your king." It is in quite common use at the present time, but not wedded to any particular hymn. In four books examined it appears with nine different hymns, no one of them being that of Watts quoted above. "Hummel" was the name of one of the early teachers of Zeuner before he came to this country. The *American Harp* was an original work of church music, and not a mere adaptation of opera airs, glees, songs, and marches. It was made up of music entirely the composition of Zeuner, with the exception of five tunes. The music seemed to catch the popular ear, as a second edition, which was really only a second printing, was called for within a year. The two tunes of Mr. Zeuner, which have been retained in most recent hymnals, were in this book—"Hummel" and "Missionary Chant." The composer states very plainly his dislike for many of the tunes which were common in his day, for he says "The church is inundated with music of a frivolous, trifling, and, may we not add, *profane* character [the italics are his]. Church music has always been believed to be a powerful means to warm and raise the heart to praise and glory to Almighty God; but much of it has become a mere mockery. It will be felt by the church as a curse not easily removed."

Charles Zeuner (1795–1857) was the compiler of four books of church music. His *Church Music*, 1831, was a collection of anthems; the *American Harp*, 1832, already referred to; the *New Village Harmony for Sabbath Schools*, and the *Ancient Lyre*, 1836. The last named was made up of the old favorites, as well as containing some new music.

HURSLEY

L. M.

PETER RITTER

The melody from which "Hursley" is taken has appeared under a number of names, in arrangements so nearly alike that they are easily recognized as having had a common origin. It has been traced back as far as a *Catholic Song Book,* printed without date some time between 1774 and 1780. A choral-book edited by Jakob and Richter in 1785 contains a setting of the melody ascribed to Peter Ritter. Mr. E. F. Rimbault stated that it was contained in a collection of manuscript music of German chorals in his possession, where it was ascribed to Ritter, and dated 1792. It is called "Framingham" (a town near Boston) in the Boston Handel and Haydn Collection, 1829. Under the name of "Halle" it is found in *Sacred Songs for Family and Social Worship,* 1842, compiled by Hastings and Mason, where it is marked as an arrangement for which copyright is claimed. The time is 7s, 6 lines, and Robinson's *Songs for the Sanctuary,* 1865, states that it was arranged by Thomas Hastings. In Ireland the tune appeared as "Stillorgan" in the *Sequel to Weyman's Melodia Sacra,* printed about 1844 in Dublin, near which there is a town called Stillorgan. The *Evangelical Hymnal,* compiled by Hall and Lazar, 1880, has the melody under the name of "Te Deum," in 7, 8, measure. The English *Church Hymnary* has it as "Pascal," set to "Rock of Ages," the first two lines being repeated to make a six-line tune.   It was first associated with the hymn of John Keble, "Sun of my soul," in a *Metrical Psalter,* issued by Henry Lahee in 1855, and later in the original edition of *Hymns Ancient and Modern,* 1861.   Hursley is the name of the parish in which the Rev. John Keble was vicar for many years.

Peter Ritter was born in Mannheim in 1760, and died there July 31, 1846.   In 1811 he was appointed chapel master to the Grand Duke of Baden.

IN HIS KEEPING

P. M.

Mrs. C. H. Morris

The hymns that will help the Christian, whether in church, parlor or kitchen, are such as Mrs. Morris writes. What more inspiring and encouraging, as well as comforting, for the housewife than to sing

> "When the early morning breaking,
> Slumber from my eyelids shaking,
> Comes the blessed thought when waking,
>   I am in His keeping.
> Day advances, labor bringing,
> Care, her mantle round me flinging,
> Yet 'midst all my soul keeps singing,
>   I am in His care.
>
> "Gentle eventide is nearing,
> Light from heaven disappearing,
> Still the blessed thought so cheering,
>   I am in His keeping.
> Now night's curtains gather 'round me,
> Yet its dangers have not found me,
> For His angel guards surround me,
>   I am in His care."

Mrs. Morris, born in 1862, believes in the old-time religion. She has made the most of the privileges that have been hers, and has used her talents in the writing of several hundred hymns. For these she prefers to write the music also, which carries them on the wings of song as she has conceived them. Her messages are for the hungry heart, the burdened spirit, and the noble strivings of Christ's devoted follower. We can almost see her as she goes about quietly doing the work in the local Methodist church in her home town of McConnellsville, Ohio, and influencing for good all who come within her sphere. Devotion is written in every line of her hymn, "Nearer, still nearer"; incitement to activity and victory in "The fight is on"; persuasion in "Let Jesus come into your heart," and peace and contentment in "Sweeter as the years go by."

ITALIAN HYMN

6, 4

FELICE GIARDINI

"Italian Hymn" is so called because it was written by an Italian. It is one of the four hymn-tunes composed at the urgent request of the Countess of Huntingdon for the collection of music prepared by Martin Madan in 1769 for the use of Lock Hospital in London, of which Mr. Madan was at that time the superintendent. It was there set to the words, which are now almost invariably used with it, "Come, thou Almighty King." The author of this hymn is unknown. It is more frequently ascribed to Charles Wesley, but there is no trustworthy evidence that he wrote it. One writer has said that, were he to guess its authorship, he would say Martin Madan. In its first setting it took its name from the name of the hymn, "A hymn to the Trinity." In English books it is usually found under the name "Moscow," from the place of Giardini's death.

Felice Giardini was born at Turin, April 12, 1716. When a boy he sang in the cathedral at Milan, but when his genius for the violin began to show itself, his father brought him back to Turin, where he was placed under the best teachers, until he became the greatest performer of his time in all Europe. He visited London in the forties, and settled there in 1850, making that city his home for the greater part of his life. He led an opera company there and also in Paris, and later took his troupe to Rus-

99

sia, where he died in Moscow, December 17, 1796. He composed much music for the harpsichord and for the violin, most of which is now forgotten. His oratorio of "Ruth" was performed several times in London, and his influence on the life of England was considerable.

KINGDOM COMING

6, 8

RIGDON McCOY McINTOSH

"The Kingdom Coming" was the title of a missionary concert exercise, printed in 1873 in a book called *The School Festival*, and as a part of it there was the hymn of Mrs. Slade, "From all the dark places of earth's heathen races," with the tune of Mr. McIntosh, which is invariably used with it. A note explained that both hymn and tune were taken from *The Amaranth*, a music book for Sunday schools, edited by R. M. MacIntosh (*sic*), and were used by his permission. The music appears also in *Good News*, another book edited by Mr. McIntosh, 1876, attributed to Emelius Larouche. In fact, there are a number of pieces of music in that book under the same name, which was merely a *nom de plume* of the editor.

Mrs. Mary Bridges Canedy Slade (1826–1882), who spent the most of her life in her native city of Fall River, Massachusetts, wrote many hymns which were set to music by Mr. McIntosh. Rigdon McCoy McIntosh (1836–1889) was an American composer and teacher, who lived in the South. He has written and composed some of the leading church hymns and tunes that have appeared in many of the church music books, especially those used in the Methodist Episcopal Church, South. He was an instructor of music in the Methodist College at Oxford, Georgia, for many years. The hymn "Gathering Home" was suggested to him as he was waiting for a train to take him to the funeral of a sister. The first two lines are his. He sent them to Mrs. Slade for completion, but the hymn was finished by her daughter, Mariana B. Slade, who has also written other hymns. The melody was written by Mrs. McIntosh. On the tombstone over the grave of Doctor McIntosh, in Oxford, Georgia, is the score of the music and the words, "In the arms of his Infinite Love."

LANCASHIRE

7, 6

HENRY SMART

"Lancashire" was written about 1836 for the hymn, "From Greenland's icy mountains," on the occasion of a missionary meeting at Blackburn, England, and appeared first in *Psalms and Hymns for Divine Worship*, 1867. Its use in American books is various and it is set to many different hymns. Perhaps the most inspiring hymn for this spirited music is Ernest W. Shurtleff's hymn beginning, "Lead on, O King Eternal." This hymn was not written until fifty years after the tune, as its inspiration was the graduation of its author from the Andover Theological Seminary in the class of 1887. Hymn and tune are used together in *The Methodist Hymnal* of 1905, and in the *New Hymnal* of the Protestant Episcopal Church, 1916. *The Church Hymnary*, published in England in 1872, contains eighteen tunes by Henry Smart, several of them being used more than once. Other tunes of his found in many American books are "Bethany," also called "Crucifer," to avoid confusion with the tune of the former name by Lowell Mason; "Smart," written for Henry Alford's hymn, "Forward be our watchword," and called in American books either "Watchword" or "Forward"; "Saint Pancras," for the church in which he was organist from 1865 to 1879. "Nachtlied" was written for the hymn, "The day is gently sinking to a close," and is generally used with it, hence its name in German form.   He wrote another tune called "Eventide," for a hymn, "The Lord be with us as we bend."   "Vexillum," meaning "banner," was written for the hymn, "Brightly beams our banner," and was first used in the appendix of the original edition of *Hymns Ancient and Modern.*

LAUDES DOMINI

6s, 6l

Joseph Barnby

This tune made its first appearance in a hymn book in 1868, in the Appendix to *Hymns Ancient and Modern.* It is also found in Barnby's collection of *Hymns with Tunes*, 1869, where it is dated 1868, and is set to the lines of the hymn, "When morning gilds the skies," whence it gets its Latin name, which is translated, "Praises to the Master."

With regard to the tunes which go to make up his collection gathered into one volume in 1869, he has this to say:

"If the outward form into which these tunes have been thrown be likely to be censured, much more so, I fancy, is the modern feeling in which they were conceived. The terms 'effeminate' and 'maudlin,' with others, are freely used nowadays to stigmatize such tunes as are not direct imitations of the old ones. And yet it had always appeared strange to me that musicians should be found who—whilst admitting that seventeenth-century tunes were very properly written in what we may call the natural idiom of that period—will not allow nineteenth-century ones to be written in the idiom of the present day. You may imitate and plagiarize the old tunes to any extent, and in all probability you will be spoken of as one who is 'thoroughly imbued with the truly devotional spirit of the old ecclesiastical writers,' but you are not permitted upon any account to give your feelings natural play; or, in short, to write spontaneously. The strangest part of the argument is this, that whilst you are urged to imitate the old works, you are warned in the same breath that to succeed is altogether without the bounds of possibility. The question then arises—would it be better, though at the risk of doing feebler things, to follow your own natural style, which, at least, would possess the merits of truth, and to leave the task of endeavoring to achieve the impossibility to those who profess it? For my part, I have elected to imitate the old writers in their independent method of working rather than their works."

For some information about Sir Joseph Barnby, see the tune "Saint Chrysostom."

LENOX

6, 8

LEWIS EDSON

The tunes of Lewis Edson have held a place in the hymnals up to very recent years, "Lenox" having been the most popular. It belongs to the class known as fugue tunes. Its most frequent setting is to the hymn of Wesley, "Blow ye the trumpet, blow." But as the taste for tunes has changed, this tune has been omitted from the books of later years.

The family of Edson was from one of the early settlers of Salem, Massachusetts, who had drifted from that town to Bridgewater, where Lewis was born January 22, 1748. He was a blacksmith by trade, and during the difficulties with England he and his family, being tories, found it desirable to remove to the sparsely settled section of western Massachusetts. Here he found names for two of his best-known tunes, "Greenfield" and "Lenox." Another one of his tunes was called "Bridgewater," from the town of his birth. These three tunes were first printed in *The Chorister's Companion*, a book of various classes of church music, where they are marked as never before printed. The date of this book is probably 1782 or 1783, there being a copy of it in the Library of Congress, in which the original owner had placed the date, 1783. It was printed for and sold by Simeon Jocelin and Amos Doolittle in New Haven, Connecticut. Lewis Edson was called "the great singer," and taught music throughout the section of western Massachusetts, New York, and Connecticut. He married in 1770, removed to New York in 1776, moved again in 1817 to Woodstock, Connecticut, where he died in the spring of 1820.

LEONI

6, 8, 4

MEYER LYON

This tune is said to be a Hebrew or Jewish melody, which was heard by Thomas Olivers while he was visiting a synagogue in 1770, and that he adapted his hymn, "The God of Abraham praise," to its meter. The words and tune were published together in 1772, and since that time the tune has been usually accompanied with these words. The hymn is a long one, divided into three parts of four stanzas each, and was first printed in a pamphlet in 1770. It is not always used with this tune. The first publication of the melody in a music collection was in a Wesleyan book, *Sacred Harmony*, in 1780. It is not in very common use, though it appeared in *The Methodist Harmonist*, 1833, but not with Oliver's hymn. It is also in *The Methodist Hymnal* of 1878. The Episcopal *Parish Hymnal* by Tucker, 1870, has it, and Hatfield's *Hymn and Tune Book*, two years later. The form of the melody in the English *Church Hymnary* differs slightly from that used in the books of this country, but it follows that found in *A Handbook of Synagogue Music for Congregational Singing*, 1889, edited by the Rev. F. L. Cohen; and Mr. Cohen states that this is the most correct form of the melody.

Meyer Lyon, whose name is generally used in its Italianized form, Leoni, was born in 1751. He had a good voice, and appeared in several of the London theaters.   He was leader of the music in the Aldgate Synagogue from 1768 to 1772, and it was here that Olivers heard the melody.   Leoni went to Dublin in 1772, where he was engaged in business, and in singing, until 1784, when he returned to London.   He next went to Jamaica, where he died in the winter of 1797.

LOVE DIVINE

8. 7. D.

JOHN ZUNDEL

In most hymnals the tune "Love Divine" is set to the hymn of Charles Wesley, beginning, "Love Divine, all loves excelling." In some books it is called "Beecher," the name of the pastor of Plymouth Church in Brooklyn, where for three different periods, covering over twenty years, John Zundel served as organist.

The composer of this tune was born in Germany, December 10, 1815. He was bandmaster of the Imperial Horse Guards in Saint Petersburg, and organist of Saint Anne's Lutheran Church in that city. His early music was written for his choir, and was sung from manuscript in that church. He came to America in 1847, and shortly after that date became associated with Henry Ward Beecher, who was striving to introduce congregational singing in his church. A small book, *Temple Melodies*, 1851, was edited by Darius E. Jones, who was then leading the music in Plymouth Church, and he was assisted by the organist. In 1855 Mr. Zundel issued his *Psalmody*, containing ninety-seven pieces of his own composition, and in the same year Mr. Beecher's *Plymouth Collection* came out, having twenty-nine tunes from the pen of his organist. Mr. Zundel wrote much music, both for instruction and for vocal use. *The Modern School for the Organ, Easy Voluntaries, Harmony and Modulation*, are some of the titles of at least a

111

dozen works that he wrote. *The Monthly Choir and Organ Journal* was established in the sixties. Following his service at Beecher's church he became organist of a church in Detroit, but after a few months he sailed for Germany, where he died in July, 1882.

LUNDIE

6. 4

THEODORE E. PERKINS

"Lundie" was the maiden name of Jane C. Bonar, with whose hymn, "Fade, fade, each earthly joy," this tune is at present mostly used. Hatfield calls it "Hope," gives its date 1858, and places it over a hymn by Henry Hope beginning, "Now have I found a friend." He also places on the same page the original version of Mrs. Bonar's hymn, whose first line was, "Pass away, earthly joy." Mr. Perkins used it in his *Sunday School Banner*, 1865. Asa Hull has a tune, the first part of which follows the melody of this one, but the last half is quite different. He uses it in his *Pilgrim's Harp*, 1869, for the hymn, "Nearer, my God, to thee," with Mrs. Bonar's hymn as a second choice. In his *Gospel Praise Book*, 1879, Mr. Hull has a tune called "Jesus is mine," resembling more closely that of Mr. Perkins, yet differing in the last few notes. This setting, Mr. Hull says, is arranged—a term employed to indicate that the melody is not original. The slurs in the last two lines seem to have been added after the tune had seen considerable service.

Theodore Edson Perkins was born July 21, 1831, in Poughkeepsie, New York, the son of a Baptist minister. His life was devoted to the upbuilding of church music, but because he did not travel much he was little known personally. He compiled many books especially for the use of Sunday schools. In

1863 his *Shining Star* appeared; the next year the *New Shining Star* was issued. Then followed *The Sacred Lute, Sabbath Carols, The Psalm King,* and the *Mount Zion Collection of Sacred and Secular Music.* Another tune by Mr. Perkins is set to the hymn of Emma Campbell, "Jesus of Nazareth passeth by."

LUTON

L. M.

Rev. George Burder

"Luton" first appeared in Aaron Williams' *Collection*, 1760, and has been quite commonly used up to recent times. In 1828 it was in the *Handel and Haydn Collection*, set to the hymn of Watts, "With all my powers of heart and tongue," and in 1849 it was in the *American Vocalist*, with this same hymn. In the *Tribute of Praise*, 1874, it was used with Blacklock's "Come, O my soul, in sacred lays," and *The Methodist Hymnal* of 1878 had it with the same hymn. It probably took its name from the town of Luton, thirty miles north of London.

George Burder was an English Congregational minister, born in London, June 5, 1752. His mother, who died when her son was four years old, was converted under the preaching of Whitefield, and when Burder was a young man he also came under the influence of the same preacher, and was further encouraged in his religious life by John Fletcher. After his marriage he removed to Coventry, where he was pastor for twenty years, and where, in 1785, he organized the first Sunday schools in that town. He was a voluminous writer, and the list of his publications in the *Dictionary of National Biography* numbers no less than twenty-five, including several volumes of *Village Sermons*, and other sermons. His *Collection of Hymns* from various authors was issued in 1784, and contained four hymns of his composi-

115

tion, and in 1806 a corrected edition of *Watts Psalms and Hymns* was issued by him. Two of his hymns were used in Hatfield's *Church Hymn Book,* 1872, and his hymn-tune "Luton" is found there twice. He was blind for the last two years of his life, died in 1832, and was buried in Bunhill Fields, where also were placed the bodies of Isaac Watts, John Bunyan, and Susannah Wesley.

LUX BENIGNA
10, 4
Rev. John Bacchus Dykes

On August 29, 1865, John B. Dykes wrote in his diary, "Began writing out a tune for 'Lead, kindly Light.'" He has also stated that the tune came to him while walking through the Strand in London. He was at that time vicar of Saint Oswald in Durham, and the tune first appeared as "St. Oswald" in *Psalms and Hymns*, edited by the Rev. D. T. Barry, and published in London in 1867. It was originally written in the key of G, but was later reset in the key of A, and used in the *Appendix to Hymns Ancient and Modern*, 1868. As it is now almost universally used with Newman's hymn, it appears under the Latin title "Lux Benigna." Newman's own comment on the popularity of his hymn was, "You see, it is not the hymn, but the tune that has gained the popularity. The tune is Dykes', and Doctor Dykes is a great master."

John Bacchus Dykes was born at Kingston-on-Hull, England, March 10, 1823. He was a scholar at Saint Catherine's, Cambridge; graduated from Cambridge University in 1847 with the degree of A.B. and received his Master's Degree three years later. He became a minor canon and precentor in Durham cathedral in 1849, where he was also the conductor of the Musical Society. He was granted the degree of Musical Doctor in 1861, and the following year became vicar of Saint Oswald, Durham.

He was a very prolific writer of church music, and many of his pieces are peculiarly fine. As one of the leaders of the new school of tune-writers, he did much toward its development. He died at Saint Leonards, January 22, 1876, at the early age of fifty-three.

MAITLAND

C. M.

GEORGE NELSON ALLEN

It frequently happens when a hymn or tune is copied from another book a wrong ascription is given. When "Maitland" was used in *The Olive Leaf*, 1878, it was erroneously said to have been written by "James Allen, of England, from the English Congregational *Hymn Book*." It was probably named for the English musician, J. A. Fuller Maitland, who wrote a life of Schumann, and several articles for Grove's *Dictionary of Music;* but it was composed by an American, George N. Allen. It is mostly used with the hymn, "Must Jesus bear the cross alone?" The first stanza follows very closely a stanza of a hymn written in 1692 by Thomas Shepherd, "Shall Simon bear the cross alone?" Both hymn and tune appeared in *The Social and Sabbath Hymn Book*, 1849, edited by Mr. Allen, and they also appear in *The Manual of Praise*, 1880, prepared by two of the professors at Oberlin, where both hymn and tune are ascribed to G. N. Allen. The tune was used in *The Plymouth Collection*, 1855, where it is called "Cross and Crown," a Western melody.

George Nelson Allen was born in Mansfield, Massachusetts, in 1812. Having studied some in Boston, he entered the Junior class at Oberlin in 1837. His knowledge of music led to his appointment as instructor of sacred music, and after graduation as professor of music in that college. To meet the demands of many of the students, he taught them outside of his college work—a plan leading to a School of Music, which was later taken into connection with the college as a Conservatory of Music. After his retirement, in 1864, he moved to Cincinnati, where he died in 1877. He is buried in Oberlin.

MARION

S. M.

Arthur H. Messiter

The tune "Marion" is generally used with the hymn of Edward H. Plumptre, "Rejoice, ye pure in heart," which was written in 1865 as a processional for a choir festival in Peterborough Cathedral. The tune dates from 1883, and was named from the mother of its composer. It was in *The Plymouth Hymnal*, compiled by Lyman Abbott in 1893, and in most of the recent hymnals.

Arthur Henry Messiter was the son of George and Marion Messiter, and was born in Frome, Somersetshire, England. He was educated at a private classical school in England, and studied music during the period from 1850 to 1855. After coming to America he settled in New York City, where he was organist and choir director for many years in Trinity Church. He prepared a new edition of *The Psalter*, pointed for singing and set to music according to the use of Trinity Parish. A committee was appointed consisting of the four organists of the parish, but he did most of the work of arranging, and his name alone appears upon the title page. He also wrote a history of the choir and music at Trinity Church, which contains also much of the history of the church itself. And as many of the prominent musicians of his day and earlier were at one time or another members of one of the four choirs of Trinity Parish, much of the musical history of New York is included in the work

121

of Mr. Messiter.   He was an excellent accompanist, and although he used plain-song sparingly, he was known as one of the most talented Gregorian players in the country.   During all of his long term of service at Trinity he felt the peculiar responsibilities of his position, and when he came to compile a hymnal, it was singularly free from unworthy compositions. He was retired on a pension in 1897, and died July 2, 1916.

MARLOW

C. M.

John Chetham

"Marlow," as used in hymnals of the present day, is a melody from the Rev. John Chetham, as altered by Lowell Mason. It is said to have first appeared in *A Book of Psalmody*, issued in London in 1718. A third edition of this book by Chetham published in London in 1724 is in the Library of Congress, and contains the melody of this tune set to the 133d psalm. There was no other name attached to it. It is also found in a later book of *Sacred Music* by John Chetham, but revised by "Mr. Stopford, organist of Halifax," and printed in 1810. In 1832 Lowell Mason introduced it into his *Choir*, and made a few changes, leaving it in the form that we now have it. No single hymn seems to have become associated with it, but it is variously used with many common-meter stanzas.

John Chetham was born about 1700, and died in August, 1763, the records of the church where he was curate showing that he was buried August 29, 1763. Only a few facts from the sixty years of his life have been found. He became master of the Clerks' School in Skipton, Yorkshire, England, in March, 1737, and curate of the church in that place in June, 1739. It is probable that he retained this position up to the time of his death in 1763. His first music book, as already stated, was published in 1718, and eleven editions of it were printed up to

1787. An enlarged and revised edition was made by Houldsworth at London in 1832. It was his ardent desire that every member of his congregation should join in the singing, and he therefore prepared his books in such a way that every voice could find a part within its compass.

MARTYN

SIMEON BUTLER MARSH

Simeon Butler Marsh was born June 1, 1798, at Weathersfield, Connecticut. He was always fond of music, and at the age of seven joined a children's choir. He later secured a music teacher, and as soon as he felt qualified began to conduct singing schools. One morning in the autumn of 1834 he was on his way from Amsterdam to Johnstown, on his weekly circuit of singing schools, when the melody of "Martyn" came to him. Dismounting his horse he jotted it down, using as the hymn that one of John Newton, beginning, "Mary at her Saviour's tomb." Then on the Sabbath, when he had taught it to his choir, this tune which he had composed was sung for the first time as a part of a divine service under the direction of the author, who was accompanying on an organ which he had built. The tune was used in the *Plymouth Collection* of Henry Ward Beecher, 1855, with the words of Newton's hymn. In 1859 another book used it to words by Robert Grant, "Saviour, when in dust to thee." Some years later Dr. Thomas Hastings discovered that the tune was better adapted to Wesley's "Jesus, Lover of my soul" than the hymn selected by Mr. Marsh. With the consent of his friend he made the change, and in all books published during the last half century "Martyn" and Wesley's words have been linked together. Mr. Marsh wrote two cantatas, some anthems, and a few other tunes, but "Martyn" is the only one that has come into common use.   For six years he was superintendent of the Sunday school in Sherburne, New York, and for three years organist and choir leader there.   The last years of his life were spent in Albany with his son, and he died there July 14, 1875.

MATERNA

C. M. D.

SAMUEL A. WARD

In hymn books of recent date this tune is used with Miss Katharine Lee Bates' hymn, "America, the beautiful." Why then should it be called "Materna," as the word "mother" does not appear in that hymn? The tune was written in 1882 and in most of the books for the thirty years following it was set to the hymn, "O mother dear, Jerusalem," which suggests the appropriateness of the name. Belden used it in his *Christ in Song*, 1900, and named it "Resurrection." It is called "Southwell" in *Hymns of the Kingdom of God*, 1910, and "Caldwell" in Bedell's *Church Hymnary*, 1892. But from present usage it seems to be destined to become the common tune for the patriotic hymn of Miss Bates. One other tune of Mr. Ward's, named "Currier," was used in *The Praise of Zion* in 1865.

The composer, Samuel Augustus Ward, was born in Newark, New Jersey, December 28, 1848. He studied music in New York City, and became a prominent figure in the musical life of his native city, where for fourteen years he was the conductor of its Orpheus Club. During the last twenty-five years of his life he had a prosperous and growing business in Newark as a dealer in pianos, music, and supplies, and was planning to add to the size of his store at the time of his death. He had resigned from the leadership of the music club at the close of the season in 1902, and lived but little more than a year after that.   His death occurred September 28, 1903, at Newark, and his funeral service was conducted by his son-in-law, the Rev. Henry W. Armstrong, an Episcopal clergyman.

MEDITATION

11, 8

FREEMAN LEWIS

Many composers are known by a single tune only.
Freeman Lewis belongs to this class. His one tune,
however, has appeared under several names. In the
Hymnal of the Seventh Day Adventists it is called
"Beloved." In the *Baptist Hymnal* of 1883 and the
Hymn and Tune Book of the Methodist Episcopal
Church, South, 1889, it is called "Dulcimer," while in
The Methodist Hymnals of 1878 and 1905 it appears
as "Meditation." In all of these books the melody is
set to the hymn of Joseph Swain, "O thou in whose
presence my soul takes delight." The United Pres-
byterian book, 1887, uses the tune under its name
"Meditation," but there it is set to other words.

Freeman Lewis (1780–1859) was the compiler of
a music book called *The Beauties of Harmony*, c.
1813, and printed in Pittsburgh. A second edition
was printed in 1816, and a third in 1818. The
library of the Western Reserve Historical Society in
Cleveland, Ohio, has a book without title page,
which appears to be substantially the same as Lewis'
Beauties of Harmony, but six pieces have been left
out and fourteen added. The preface is dated in
Fayette County, Pennsylvania, October 1, 1828, and
Mr. Lewis writes, "I have another volume of about
two hundred pages nearly ready for the press in
which will be found some things relative to music not
hitherto published in the Western country." It does

129

not appear, however, that such a book ever saw the light of print.   All of his books were published with shaped notes, a common style west of the Alleghanies. Freeman was a competent surveyor of Uniontown, who started in 1850 to write a history of Fayette County, but he never completed it.

MERTON

C. M.

Henry K. Oliver

"Merton" is a tune that has about passed out of use. It was used in *The Methodist Hymnal* of 1878, and Charles S. Robinson has it in *Laudes Domini*, 1887. The name was probably suggested by one of the oldest colleges in Oxford—Merton College. Its composition enforces the truth that when a tune comes to mind it must be put into permanent form or it is lost. Oliver was organist in Salem from 1828 to 1849, and one Sunday in 1843 the tune "Merton" was born. Its story is thus told by Henry M. Brooks, in his book, *Old Time Music*. The hymn to close the afternoon service was Doddridge's "Ye golden lamps of heaven, farewell." Mr. Oliver could think of no tune for it which suited him, and the sermon was getting on toward its close when the melody of this tune came into his mind. He prepared a copy for his own use, and furnished each one of the singers with his part of the score, and the new tune was sung with earnestness and effect. The next day when the pastor met him he asked about the new tune, and was told how it was composed during the time of the sermon. He was not pleased that his organist should occupy his time in this fashion, instead of listening to the lessons of the sermon. But "suppose," replied Mr. Oliver, "that while we were leading the worship at our end of the church, some new thought, which had not occurred to you during your work on your sermon in your study, should suddenly suggest itself to you. Would you not just quietly pencil it down on the margin of your notes, so we, the people, might have the benefit of it?" And as he had to confess that he had done that many times, the composer asked, "Whose notes are more sinful—yours of the margin or mine of the score?"

MISSIONARY CHANT

L. M.

CHARLES ZEUNER

"I ran home as fast as ever I could and put it on paper before I should forget it," and he goes on to explain how "Missionary Chant" was written: "I was sitting on one of those seats on Boston Common on a most beautiful moonlight night, all alone, with all the world moving about me, when suddenly 'Missionary Chant' was given me." It first appeared in his *American Harp*, 1832, set to "Ye Christian heroes, go proclaim," later changed to "Ye Christian heralds, go proclaim." This setting is retained in the Episcopal *New Hymnal*, but no hymn is used with it exclusively. It is found with such missionary hymns as "Jesus shall reign where'er the sun," and "Kingdoms and thrones to God belong."

The composer was born September 20, 1795, in Eisleben, Germany, and was christened Heinrich Christopher Zeuner; but upon coming to this country in 1824 he assumed the name of Charles. Soon after his arrival in Boston he became organist in the Park Street Church, then organist for the Handel and Haydn Society in 1830, and was its president for a few months. A few years later he removed to Philadelphia, where he held positions as organist in Saint Anne's Episcopal Church and the Arch Street Presbyterian Church. Mr. Zeuner composed an oratorio, "The Feast of Tabernacles," which was presented in Boston for eight evenings, but it was a

133

financial failure, and he attempted to destroy all the copies he could find. A few, however, were saved. Zeuner was never married, and was without relatives in this country. On November 7, 1857, he left his home in Philadelphia, and shortly afterward his body was found in the woods with unmistakable evidence of suicide.

MORNINGTON

S. M.

The Earl of Mornington

Garrett Colley Wellesley, the Earl of Mornington, was born at Dangan, Ireland, July 19, 1735. Like most musicians, he early displayed his aptitude for music and with little assistance from outside sources he taught himself to play the violin and the organ, and began to compose. When he sought the instruction of two noted teachers he was told that he already knew all that they could have taught him. He graduated from Dublin University as a Bachelor in 1754, and three years later gained the degree of Master. His degree of Doctor of Music was conferred in 1764 and he became the first professor of music in his Alma Mater the same year, a position he held for ten years, when he resigned. He was made Viscount Wellesley and Earl of Mornington in 1760, succeeding his father, who had been created Baron Mornington in 1746. Three of his sons were known later as Richard, Marquis Wellesley; Arthur, Duke of Wellington; and Henry, Lord Cowley. He died at Kensington, May 22, 1781.

Most of his compositions were vocal. He excelled as a writer of glees, madrigals, and catches. These were issued in single parts, but a complete collection of them has been made by H. R. Bishop. Some of his music was written for the church, and copies of them are said to exist in the choir books of Saint Patrick's Cathedral in Dublin. A chant in

E is widely known. It was arranged as a short meter hymn-tune, "Mornington," and appeared in Miller's *David's Harp,* 1805, and Lowell Mason introduced it into his first publication, the *Boston Handel and Haydn Society's Collection of Church Music,* in 1828. From that source it has had an extended circulation in hymn books.

NAOMI

C. M.

Hans G. Naegali

"Naomi" was another of the tunes which Lowell Mason brought with him on his return from his trip to Europe, and he published it in a music periodical called *Occasional Psalm and Hymn Tunes,* in 1836. It is found in Mason's *Carmina Sacra,* or *Boston Collection of Church Music,* 1841, without any composer's name, and set to the hymn, "Father, whate'er of earthly bliss," and from that book it was copied extensively into other books. Its popularity in 1893 is indicated by the fact that it was omitted from only a single one of the thirty American hymn books which were made the basis of the *National Hymn Book* published in that year, and in all of them it was set to Anne Steele's hymn, "Father, whate'er of earthly bliss."

Hans G. Naegali (1768–1836) was a Swiss writer, printer, and seller of music. He published much of Beethoven's music, including three of his grand solo sonatas. An interesting story is told of him that he actually succeeded in interpolating four measures into one of the movements of a Beethoven sonata. The great master must, however, have pardoned the crime, for his later letters to the publisher were couched in terms of affection, and he did his utmost to induce the Archduke Rodolph to subscribe to a volume of Naegali's poems, printed in 1824. This Swiss writer composed many pieces of choral music,

137

founded and became president of the Swiss Association for the cultivation of music, and published a book on *The Teachings of the Song on the Principles of Pestalozzi*. One of his songs, under the title, "Life let us cherish," was for a long time popular in England.   A monument to his memory was erected in Zurich in 1848.

NATIONAL HYMN

10s

GEORGE WILLIAM WARREN

This tune for a national hymn was written for the Centennial in 1876. It was introduced into the Episcopal *Hymnal* in 1892, set to the hymn, "God of our fathers, whose almighty hand." In 1894 it had appeared in Tucker's edition of the *Hymnal*, marked as one contributed to that book. The Presbyterian *Hymnal* of 1895 used it, and placed the date, 1892, over it to indicate its first appearance in a hymn book. The composer contributed two other tunes to this edition of the Presbyterian *Hymnal*, one of which was called "Easter Angels" and the other "Log College." The latter tune was written December 5, 1894, for a hymn by Dr. Louis F. Benson, beginning, "O thou whose feet have climbed life's hill," and both hymn and tune were used in the Presbyterian *Hymnal* of 1895, of which Doctor Benson was one of the editors. The title is reminiscent of the Log College of William Tennant, founded in 1728. The "National Hymn" was used in the second edition of Bishop Darlington's *Hymnal*, 1897, but is there called "Columbia."

George William Warren was born in Albany, August 17, 1828. His love of the organ and his passion for music led him to devote his life to that work. From 1846 to 1858 he served as organist of Saint Peter's Church in his native city. He then filled a like position in the Church of the Holy

Trinity in Brooklyn, where he was during the sixties, and later he accepted the place as organist and director of the music at Saint Thomas' Church in New York City. While there he published, in 1888, Warren's *Hymns and Tunes* as sung at Saint Thomas' Church. He died in 1902.

NETTLETON

8, 7

JOHN WYETH

"Hallelujah" is the original name of the tune "Nettleton," as it appears in Part II of Wyeth's *Repository*, 1813. The tune is there written in the key of F, and in common time, and took its title from the refrain, "Hallelujah, hallelujah, we are on our journey home." Just when the time and title were changed I have been unable to discover, but about half of the modern hymnals attribute it to Asahel Nettleton and the rest to John Wyeth. Nettleton compiled a volume of *Village Hymns* in 1824, but there were no tunes in this book, and it is doubtful if he had anything to do with the tune. It is usually set to the words of Robert Robertson, "Come, thou Fount of every blessing."

John Wyeth was a native of Massachusetts, born at Cambridge, March 31, 1770. He learned the business of a printer, and upon attaining his majority went to San Domingo to superintend a large printing establishment. Later he returned to this country, lived for awhile in Philadelphia, and in 1792 went to Harrisburg, where he connected himself with the newspaper, *The Oracle of Dauphin*, which he successfully carried on until 1827. He was postmaster of Harrisburg from 1793 to 1798. Upon retiring from business he removed to Philadelphia, where he died January 23, 1858.

John Wyeth's *Repository of Sacred Music* first

appeared in 1810, and continued to be reprinted in various editions, the fifth being dated 1820. Afterward two stereotype editions were issued in 1826 and 1834, these being copyrighted in 1826. A *Supplement*, called the Second Part, was issued with tunes intended especially for the Methodist Church. This part came out in 1813, and more than one third of the tunes were original, his "Hallelujah" being included in that number.

NEWBOLD

C. M.

George Kingsley

"Newbold" was composed by George Kingsley, and probably first appeared in his book, *The Harp of David*, 1847, for he introduces it into a later book, *Templi Carmina*, 1853, and states that it is from *The Harp of David*. Here it is found on page 94, set to the words, "O praise the Lord, for he is good."

George Kingsley was born in Northampton, Massachusetts, July 7, 1811, and at an early age showed his bent toward music. Through his own exertions he acquired a remarkable mastery of the science of music, and learned to play both the organ and the piano. At the age of eighteen he became known as an organist in one of the churches in Hartford, Connecticut. He served as organist in the Old South Church, and the Hollis Street Church, in Boston. For ten years he was teacher of music in Girard College, Philadelphia, and also had charge of the music in the public schools of that city, then he went to New York and Brooklyn, where he continued his work. He published a number of musical books, some in his own name, and others in conjunction with Lowell Mason. His earliest compilation was *The Harmonist*, printed in Boston in 1833, when he was only twenty-two years old. Others were *The Social Choir*, 1836; *The Harp of David*, 1843 (first edition); *The Young Ladies' Harp*, 1847; *Templi Carmina*, 1853; and the *Juvenile Choir*, 1865.

George Kingsley died March 14, 1884, and at the musical service held the next Sabbath evening at the church which he attended in Northampton all the music used was of his composition, and this tune was one of the number.

NICÆA

11, 12, 12, 10

John Bacchus Dykes

This tune was written for the hymn with which it is generally used, "Holy, holy, holy," and was first inserted in the original edition of *Hymns Ancient and Modern*, 1861. The historical edition of that popular English hymn book states that it was probably inspired "by a tune of John Hopkins, called 'Trinity,' set to this same hymn in 1850."

Doctor Dykes (1823–1876) began to play the organ in his grandfather's church when he was ten years old. He conducted a Musical Society while he was an undergraduate at Cambridge, and in 1849 he became precentor at Durham Cathedral. While there he directed for some years an amateur choral society, which met at the homes of the members in turn. During Lent their practice was restricted to sacred music, but at other times secular music was introduced, and the ancient piece of Orlando Gibbons, "The Silver Swan," was almost always upon their program. His contributions to *Hymns Ancient and Modern* were many and continuous. For the first edition he furnished seven tunes; for the appendix, twelve; for the second edition, twenty, making thirty-nine that were written especially for this book, and there were sixteen more included from other sources. He was married in 1850 and took his bride to live at Hollingside Cottage, about a mile out from Durham. His tune of this name is reminiscent of

145

his home.   Doctor Fowler's life of Dykes has this comment: "On June 1st, 1859, Doctor Dykes visited the Rev. John Sharp at Horbury, and preached there.   The special object of this visit was to make his first confession.   The hymn-tune, which he called 'Horbury,' was written at this time, and it was to him a perpetual reminder of the peace and comfort he found then."

OLD HUNDRED

L. M.

GUILLIAME FRANC

The first appearance of the tune now known as "Old Hundred" is in a Huguenot Psalter, printed in Geneva in 1551. It was introduced into England in Daye's Psalter, twelve years later, 1563. In the version of the Psalms made by Sternhold and Hopkins, and published in 1605, the tune appears set to the words of William Kethe, "All people that on earth do dwell." But in each of the six Methodist hymn books published in America with tunes it appears set to the words of Watts, "Before Jehovah's awful throne," which are printed in late editions of his Psalms as the second part of Psalm 100, a proper recognition of the name. In the Genevan Psalter the tune is set to the 134th psalm, but when introduced among English-speaking peoples it was used with the 100th. It is also frequently called "Savoy," for the reason that it was used by a Huguenot congregation established in the Savoy, London, during the reign of Queen Elizabeth.

The name of Guilliame Franc is usually associated with this music as its composer. He was a Frenchman, born in Rouen about 1520, who established a school of music in Geneva in 1541. In the following year he was appointed a member of the choir, and master of the children of Saint Peter's Church. About 1545 he left Geneva and joined the choir at Lausanne, and died at that place in May, 1570. It

147

is said that he did a great share of the work in preparing the music for the Psalter of 1551, and he also prepared another musical edition of the Psalms after he had removed to Lausanne, and it was printed at Geneva. A monograph giving all the facts then obtainable about this old tune was published in 1854 by William H. Havergal.

OLIVET

6, 4

The tune "Olivet" was written by Lowell Mason for the hymn of Ray Palmer, "My faith looks up to thee." Both hymn and tune are distinctively American in their origin. Mr. Palmer had written his hymn about 1830, but it had never been used as such, and it is doubtful if anyone except the author had seen it. Two years later, when Mr. Mason and Thomas Hastings were preparing a book called *Spiritual Hymns for Social Worship,* Mr. Mason asked his friend if he did not have some poems that he could use as hymns in the new book. The hymn was produced, and the tune "Olivet" was composed for it, and appeared in the book published in 1832. Since then both hymn and tune have come into almost universal use in hymn books, and they seem to be wedded to each other.

Lowell Mason was a native of Medfield, Massachusetts, where he was born January 8, 1792. For his life-work he began banking, locating in Savannah, Georgia, and spending fourteen years in that place. There he served as organist, led the choir, and made a collection of music. Returning to his home State, his collection was issued in 1822, anonymously, as the *Handel and Haydn Collection of Sacred Music.* It was a great success, and book after book of other music was issued, and Mr. Mason had found his place in the musical world. Boston then became his home,

149

and one result of his earnest efforts was accomplished when he succeeded in having music introduced as a study in the schools of that city in 1838.   He later removed to New York, where his sons had established a music publishing business, and still later to Orange, New Jersey, where he died, August 11, 1872, at the age of eighty.

PENTECOST

L. M.

REV. WILLIAM BOYD

"Pentecost" has stood the test of time, for it is the only one of *Thirty-two Hymn Tunes* composed by members of the University of Oxford, published in 1868, that is still in common use. In a statement made for the London *Musical Times* in 1908, Mr. Boyd says: "Baring-Gould asked me to compose a tune to 'Come, Holy Ghost, our souls inspire,' to be sung at a large meeting of Yorkshire colliers. I walked, talked, slept and ate with the words, and at last evolved the tune which I naturally named 'Pentecost.'" "How came it to be associated with 'Fight the good fight'? Ah, that is a funny thing. One day as I was walking along Fleet Street I felt a slap on my back, and turning round I saw my dear old friend, Arthur Sullivan. He asked for the use of the tune in *Church Hymns*, which he was then editing. 'All right,' I said, 'send me a checque and I agree.'" No copy of the book was sent him, much less a proof, and he was horrified to find that Sullivan had assigned it to "Fight the good fight." It struck the popular favor, and in nearly every book in which it is now introduced at least one of the settings is to this hymn of Monsell. Whenever his permission is asked for the use of the tune, he insists that it be used with this hymn. He prepared a facsimile to be printed in the *Musical Times*, and as the air is made on only five consecutive tones, he said, "I will write

151

the heading Pen-tecost because Pen is the first syllable of my wife's name, and she is very fond of the tune." The Rev. William Boyd was vicar of All Saints Church, Norfolk Square, Hyde Park, from 1893 until his retirement a few years ago. He died in the latter part of 1927.

PILGRIMS

11, 10

Henry Smart

He who would sing Faber's hymn, "Hark, hark, my soul," finds in most hymn books a choice of two tunes. In his own collection of hymns, 1861, Faber called it "The pilgrims of the night," and so when Henry Smart wrote a tune to it for the appendix to *Hymns Ancient and Modern,* 1868, it was natural that he should use the first noun of this title for the name of his tune. Both hymn and tune are very popular and are found in most books of recent date. The other tune found with this hymn is "Angels' Song," by John B. Dykes.

Henry Smart was an English composer, born in London, October 26, 1813. His father, who bore the same name, was the inventor of one form of the metronome. The son also had great skill in making mechanical contrivances. He tried to study law but was not successful in its continuance, so he turned to music. As his father had been a manufacturer of pianos and organs, so the son became an authority on the organ, and several large ones were erected after his specifications. He composed a sacred cantata, entitled "Jacob," for the musical festival in Glasgow in 1873, and many sacred songs and duets which belong more properly to the realm of domestic music. One English writer states that "Smart's original hymn-tunes are excellent examples of pure English melody, and perhaps with one exception

153

they never present any of the trivial and sugary features which disfigure many (though not all) of the Barnby and Dyke school." Smart did not approve of the Gregorian melodies in general use in his day, and even referred to them as meaningless and uncouth.   He died July 6, 1879.

PILOT

7s, 61

JOHN E. GOULD

"Pilot" was written in 1872 for a special Sunday-school occasion, and was printed in *The Sabbath,* 1873, compiled by Charles Everest, where it is set to the first stanza of the hymn, "Jesus, Saviour, pilot me." Edward Hopper, who wrote the hymn, was pastor of the Church of the Sea and Land in New York City. The hymn, consisting of six stanzas, was first published in 1871, and in 1878 the Rev. Charles S. Robinson took the first, fifth, and sixth stanzas as a hymn in his *Spiritual Songs.* It is always associated with the tune "Pilot."

John Edgar Gould was the son of Captain Horace Gould and Mary Allen, and was born in Bangor, Maine, in 1820. When thirty years old he went to New York and opened a music store on Broadway. He had written considerable music before this date, and with Edward L. White had issued several books, *The Modern Harp,* 1846; *The Wreath of School Songs* and *The Tyrolien Lyre* in 1847; and *The Sunday School Lute,* 1848. Under his own name he published four books, including *Harmonia Sacra,* 1851, and *Songs of Gladness for the Sabbath School,* 1869. He married Josephine Barrows, of Bergen Heights, New Jersey, and lived in that town for awhile; then he went to Philadelphia, where he had a music store. In September, 1874, he left this country for a trip to England and the Continent, but his health declined, instead of being improved, and while in Algiers he died on March 4, 1875.   Another tune, "Bera," is used in present-day hymnals, and with many other tunes of his composition appeared in his *Songs of Gladness*.   Most of these are now forgotten, and only the two mentioned remain in use to preserve his name.

RATHBUN

8, 7

There is a little town in Pennsylvania called Rathbun, and it is probable that Ithamar Conkey's tune was named from it. The date of its composition is variously given as 1847 and 1851. The earliest publication of it that I have found is in Greatorex's *Collection of Church Music*, 1851, where it is set to the hymn of William A. Muhlenberg, "Saviour, who thy flock art feeding." In more recent hymnals it is invariably placed with the hymn of John Bowring, "In the cross of Christ I glory." It is such a popular tune that some books have it more than once, but seldom is it contained in any book without one setting to this hymn of Bowring. A soldier once rode into a village in Africa and asked for food, but it was denied him. He had ridden a long distance, and he must rest his horse before starting back, so he sat down and began to sing, "In the cross of Christ I glory." The tune caught the ear of the chief; he sent for food and treated the soldier kindly, for that was a missionary tune, and the missionaries had been kind to the natives.

The composer's name is found in the earlier hymn books as J. Conkey, or John Conkey. But as further knowledge grew, his true name of Ithamar Conkey became better known. He was born in 1815 in the little town of Shutesbury in western Massachusetts. His musical life was spent in the city of New York,

157

where he was at various times connected with choirs in Calvary Church, Grace Church, and in 1861 he was basso and conductor of the quartet choir in the Madison Avenue Baptist Church. Some other tunes of his have been printed, but "Rathbun" is the one by which he will be remembered. He died in 1867.

REGENT SQUARE

8, 7, 61

Henry Smart

"Regent Square" received its name from Regent Street in London, where stood Saint Philip's Church, in which Henry Smart was the organist in 1838 and 1839. Its first appearance was in *Psalms and Tunes for Divine Worship*, published in London in 1867. It was introduced into *The Methodist Hymnal* in 1878, where it is set to the words, "O thou God of my salvation."

Henry Smart, born in 1813 in London, was the son of another Henry, who was a violinist and a piano manufacturer, and when the son tried to study law, but did not find it to his liking, it was only natural that he should turn to the organ. His connection with psalmody began with his appointment as organist of the parish church at Blackburn in 1831. From Blackburn he went to London, where he spent the remainder of his life as organist in the churches of that city. For four years he presided at the organ of Saint Philip's Presbyterian Church, then for twenty years, 1844–1864, he was at Saint Luke's. He was married in 1840 in Saint Pancras Church, and in 1865 was invited to play the organ there. During all the period of his service in this church he was blind. He composed an anthem for the centenary of the Reformation. Many of his hymn-tunes were composed during the sixties and appeared in *Psalms and Hymns for Divine Worship*,

159

published in 1867 for the use of the English Presbyterians. He died in London, July 6, 1879, within a month from the announcement that Queen Victoria had granted him a Civil List pension of one hundred pounds per year in recognition of his services to music.

RESCUE THE PERISHING
11, 10
WILLIAM HOWARD DOANE

The hymn "Rescue the perishing" was written by Fanny Crosby at the suggestion of Mr. Doane, and first appeared with his tune in 1870 in his *Songs of Devotion*. This book was printed just as the issuing of copyrights was transferred from the District Courts to the Librarian of Congress, so it was copyrighted in the office of the clerk of the District Court for the Southern District of Ohio, and also in the office of the Librarian of Congress. Fifty-four of its tunes appear with the monogram **WHD**, and several others have the full name of Mr. Doane over them. This tune was recopyrighted in 1898 for another period of twenty-eight years.

William Howard Doane was born February 3, 1832, at Preston, Connecticut. His first piece of music was written in 1848, and was dedicated to his cousin, Miss Fannie Mary Treat, who became his wife in 1857. He entered business in Norwich as a cotton manufacturer, and after representing his firm for a few years in Chicago he removed to Cincinnati, Ohio, where he became the head of a large wood-working business, and he carried it on successfully for many years, inventing much of the machinery which was used in the industry. He began to write hymn-tunes after recovering from a sickness in 1862, and set to music many of the hymns of Fanny Crosby, including "Jesus, keep me near the cross," "I am

Thine, O Lord," and "Pass me not." He served for twenty-five years as superintendent of the Sunday school in Mount Auburn, Ohio, was an active member of the Baptist Church, and gave of his wealth to endow the library in Denison University, Granville, Ohio. He died December 24, 1915, at South Orange, New Jersey.

RUSSIAN HYMN

P. M.

Alexis F. Lvoff

The Russian national hymn dates from 1833. The emperor then expressed a desire to his court musician that one should be composed. Lvoff writes in his memoir: "I felt the necessity of composing what would be majestic, powerful, full of sentiment, comprehensible to all, suitable to the army and suitable to the people, from the learned to the illiterate. All these conditions frightened me, and at first I could compose nothing. One night, on returning to my quarters at a very late hour, I composed and wrote out the tune on the spur of the moment." After suitable words had been furnished by Joulowsky, the emperor and empress and the Grand Duke Michael went on November 23 to the Court Chapel to hear it. The whole choir was supported by two orchestras. "The sovereign ordered the hymn to be played over several times, and asked to hear it sung without accompaniment; then he had it played by each orchestra in turn, and finally by the united body of performers. His Majesty then said to me in French, 'It is really superb,' and there and then ordered that the minister of war be informed that the hymn was adopted for the army. This measure was officially ratified December 4, 1833. The first public performance took place December 11." Then the composer adds a personal note: "The sovereign graciously presented to me a gold snuff box, and ordered

163

that the words, 'God protect the Czar' (the first line of the anthem's text), should be added to the armorial bearings of the Lvoff family.   The name of the composer is written both Lwoff and Lvov.   A copy of the music of the hymn with Russian words, in the Library of Congress, has an autograph presentation "de la part du compositeur, A. de Lvoff."

SAINT GERTRUDE

6, 5, D.

ARTHUR SEYMOUR SULLIVAN

"Saint Gertrude" was named for Mrs. Gertrude Clay-Ker-Seymer, the sister-in-law of Frederick Clay, and was probably written at her home at Hanford, Dorsetshire, where Sir Arthur frequently stopped for several weeks at a time. It was sung in the private chapel of that home, Sullivan playing the harmonium, and teaching the family the tune. It was first printed in the *Musical Times* for December, 1871, though it was written for the *Church Hymnary* published in 1872. It was composed for the hymn of Sabine Baring-Gould, "Onward, Christian soldiers." In some books there are extra notes in the tenor of the refrain over the word "war." These were not in the original form, but were added subsequently, and appeared in the version of the tune that was used in *Church Hymns*, 1874, of which Sullivan was the first musical editor. The writing of "Saint Gertrude" was really one of the results of a quarrel. The quarrel was between the proprietors of *Hymns Ancient and Modern* and the firm of Novello, who printed it, and who finally gave way to Messrs. Clowes, the publishers of the numerous editions issued since that time. The firm of Novello then proceeded to compile a collection of church music for which this tune was written. Sullivan had assisted a great deal in harmonizing the tunes for the Rev. Thomas Helmore's *Hymnal Noted*, and the knowledge and experience which he thus gained in regard to hymn-tunes were of material value to him in preparing his big collection for the Society for the Promotion of Christian Knowledge. The tune "Saint Gertrude" was introduced into the author's "Te Deum," written as a thanksgiving piece at the close of the Boer War in South Africa.

SAINT LOUIS

8, 6. D.

Lewis H. Redner

One of the beautiful Christmas hymns is that of Bishop Phillips Brooks, "O little town of Bethlehem," and as the music first used with it was composed especially for it, both hymn and tune are always found together. Phillips Brooks had visited the Holy Land, and had walked in the town of the Saviour's birth. In 1868, when rector of the Church of the Holy Trinity, in Philadelphia, he wrote this carol for the Christmas service of the Sunday school. Lewis H. Redner was the organist of the church, the superintendent of the Sunday school, and a teacher of one of its classes, and was therefore asked to furnish a tune for the new hymn. The melody of the music came to the composer during Saturday night, and the harmonies were completed for the Sunday service. It was afterward published as a pamphlet and offered for sale. The first appearance in a hymn book was in *The Church Porch*, a Service Book and Hymnal for Sunday Schools, compiled and edited by William R. Huntington, rector of All Saints Church in Worcester, Massachusetts, 1874. He it was who gave it the name of Saint Louis. Slowly it came into public notice; in 1892 it was introduced into the Episcopal Hymnal, and it now finds a place in most denominational hymn books.

Phillips Brooks was born in Boston, December 13, 1835, graduated from Harvard in 1855, and studied for the ministry in the seminary at Alexandria, Virginia.   After a few years as rector in Philadelphia, he went to Boston, where for more than twenty years Trinity Church, under his ministry, became the best known Episcopal church in that city.   In 1891 he was elected bishop, an office which he filled for only two years.   He died January 23, 1893.

SAINT MARTIN'S

C. M.

WILLIAM TANS'UR

"Saint Martin's" tune first appeared in the second edition of *The Royal Melody Compleat, or the New Harmony of Sion*, London, 1740, marked "Composed in four parts: W. T."

Note the apostrophe in the surname of William Tans'ur. Just why it is there and what it means has never been explained. The date and place of the birth of this musician are in doubt. Sir George Grove, in his *Musical Dictionary*, writes that it is variously stated that he was born in 1699 at Barnes in Surrey, or in 1700 at Dunchurch in Warwickshire. He was of a roving disposition, holding classes in the different places that he visited, and serving as organist in Barnes, Ewell, Leicester, and Saint Neot's. He was occupied some time in Leicester as a book-seller. He compiled and edited a number of music books, the first being *The Royal Melody*, already noted, which he himself calls "the most curiousest [*sic*] book that ever was published." One of the tunes from the second edition of this book was "Saint Martin's," and it was introduced into the first music book printed in America with notes, *The Grounds and Rules of Music*, 1721, by Thomas Walter. The first music book printed in this country was by John Tufts, but "Saint Martin's" was not in Tufts' book. One of the early printers of music books was Daniel Bayley, of Newburyport. His plan was to take from the books that came to his notice such parts as were suited to his purpose, and omit the rest. Thus one of his reprints contains a large part of *The Royal Melody* of Tans'ur, which had been printed in England in 1754. In his *New Musical Grammar*, 1746, he styles himself "Musico Theorico." He died at Saint Neot's, October 7, 1783.

SAINT THOMAS

S. M.

AARON WILLIAMS

The tune "Saint Thomas" has been ascribed to both Handel and Aaron Williams. It is a curious fact that in the four Methodist books, *The Methodist Harmonist*, 1833, gives Handel as its composer; the revision of 1837 has the name of A. Williams set over it; the Hymnal of 1878 reverts to Handel; and that of 1905 again to Aaron Williams.

Aaron Williams was of Welsh descent, but was born in England in 1731. He was a teacher of psalmody, an engraver of music, and a publisher of books. For a time he was clerk of the Scotch church at London Wall. He died in 1776 at the age of forty-five years. At least three collections of music were issued by him. *The Universal Psalmodist* was printed before 1766, for the third edition was advertised in another book printed in the latter year. This had an introduction and a collection of hymn-tunes, and sold for four shillings. Mr. Williams had issued before that year "Psalmody in Miniature containing the tenor and bass of all the tunes generally sung in public worship neatly engraved on forty-eight plates so small that the whole will conveniently lie in a common Psam [*sic*] Book. Price sixpence." It was issued in three parts, and later two supplements were added. *The Royal Harmony, or The Beauties of Church Music* was a book of one hundred and two pages and contained thirty anthems set by

171

A. Williams.   It was printed in London in 1766 from
engraved plates.   A copy of the *Universal Psalmodist* soon came to this country, and in 1769 portions of it were reprinted by Daniel Bayley at Newburyport.   This is now a rare volume, and in 1916
a copy of it was offered for sale for twenty-five dol-
lars.

SESSIONS

L. M.

Luther O. Emerson

The tune "Sessions" was written in 1847 at Salem, Massachusetts, by Luther O. Emerson, and named for his pastor, the Rev. Alexander A. Sessions. The story of its composition is thus told by its author: "One pleasant summer Sabbath day, after returning from church, being alone in my house, I took up my hymn book, and on opening it my eyes fell upon the hymn beginning, 'Sinner, O why so thoughtless grown?' My attention was at once fixed upon it. I read the whole hymn through several times, and the impression it made upon me grew stronger and stronger at each repetition. I had a longing to give expression in some way to my emotions. After a season of prayer I went to the piano, and at once played the tune just as it came to me. There was no hesitancy about it, no effort was made. I played it again and again, and felt at the time it had life-giving power, and would live."

Luther Orlando Emerson was born August 3, 1820, in Parsonfield, Maine. He was from the same family as Ralph Waldo Emerson, their grandfathers having been first cousins. Removing to Massachusetts, he taught music and led a choir in Salem for eight years. In 1844 he became organist of the Bulfinch Place Church in Boston, remaining there for four years and going from thence to the Congregational church in Greenfield. He assisted in compiling over seventy collections of music.   In a letter to the writer in 1911 he writes, "I am nearing the ninety-first milestone in my journey through this beautiful world toward the Beautiful Land of Beulah.   Should I live to see the third of August I shall reach that point."   He even passed his ninety-fifth milestone, as he died September 29, 1915.

SILOAM

C. M.

Isaac B. Woodbury

"Siloam" appeared in the *Boston Musical Education Society's Collection of Church Music*, 1842, of which Isaac B. Woodbury was one of the compilers, with Benjamin F. Baker the president of the society. On the title page of that book he is entered as organist at the Odeon, which was the meeting place of the society. It was set to the hymn of Reginald Heber, "By cool Siloam's shady rill," which accounts for the name of the tune, and music and words are now universally linked in use.

Isaac B. Woodbury was born in Beverly, Massachusetts, and when he had reached manhood he built himself a home in the near-by town of Wenham overlooking the beautiful lake there. At the age of twenty he joined the Bay State Club, which gave concerts throughout New England. At Bellows Falls he met John W. Moore, who was deeply interested in music, and who later published an *Encyclopedia of Music*, and was prevailed upon to organize an association which was called the New Hampshire and Vermont Musical Association. He was its conductor for a number of years. He taught music for awhile in Boston in connection with Benjamin F. Baker, and compiled several collections of sacred music. In 1851 he visited Europe, returning with much music for use in his books. The later years of his short life were spent in New York, where he edited several collections for church and Sunday-school usage. In 1858 he started on a trip South as a rest from the confining duties of his business. His health did not improve, and he was unable to go any farther than Columbia, South Carolina, where he died October 26, 1858, at the age of thirty-nine.

SILVER STREET

S. M.

ISAAC SMITH

Isaac Smith, the composer of "Silver Street," may
have been a well-known man of his time, but the facts
about him that have come down to us are very few.
He was born in London about 1735, and died about
1800. He was clerk, that is, choir leader, to the
Alie Street Meeting, Goodman's Fields, one of the
Nonconformist chapels in London, and is said to have
been the first Dissenting clerk to have received a
salary of as much as twenty pounds a year for his
services. Later, we are told, he was in a respectable
line of business, though just what that was is not
indicated. The London Directories for 1780 and
subsequent years show one Isaac Smith a linen
draper, while another was a grocer and tea dealer.
The musician may have been either one of these.
Having a taste for music, our writer composed and
published a number of psalm-tunes, which were in
general use among Dissenters, while some of them
were adopted by churches of other creeds. The title
of his book is, "*A Collection of Psalm Tunes* in three
parts, adapted to each measure as now sung in several churches, chapels, and meeting houses in and
about London, to which are added two anthems and
two canons. By Is. Smith." Like most English
books it was printed without date, but as the fifth
edition was published in 1790, it is thought that the
first should be dated about 1770. It is of interest to

note that the instructions for singing are given in English instead of in Italian, as was usual in that time.   His most popular tune, "Abridge," was number one in his collection.   "Silver Street" is found in some of the older hymn books as "Falcon Street."

SOUND THE BATTLE CRY

WILLIAM F. SHERWIN

William F. Sherwin wrote music for many moods; some were devotional, like "Break thou the bread of life"; some rest the soul with their quiet melodies, as "Evening Praise," with its hymn, "Day is dying in the west"; while others stir to action like a "Battle Cry." Both hymn and tune were written in 1869, and were printed in *Bright Jewels*, a book compiled by Robert Lowry. Another song, of which Mr. Sherwin wrote both words and tune in 1876, has this chorus, suggested by the words of Paul:

> "Hear the call, O gird your armor on,
> Grasp the Spirit's mighty sword;
> Take the helmet of salvation,
> Pressing on to battle for the Lord."

Sherwin's life was full of action. He was the music laureate for Chautauqua, writing songs for the classes from 1874 to 1878. He assisted in compiling several music books, *The Victory*, 1869, with Chester G. Allen; *Songs of Grace and Glory*, with Silas J. Vail, and *Chautauqua Carols*, 1878, with Robert Lowry, in which he wrote twenty or more songs for that summer meeting. Then in 1881 he issued *Heart and Voice for Sunday Schools*. He was professor in a female academy, received musical instruction from Lowell Mason and George J. Webb, and displayed such ability in conducting that he entered into the faculty of the numerous conventions that were held

179

in various parts of the country. He often led the morning services held the hour before breakfast at the Chautauqua Assemblies, and the congregation went away encouraged for the day's duties by his hymn, "Why is thy faith, O child of God, so small?"

SPOHR

C. M. D.

Louis Spohr

This tune is arranged from an air and chorus in Spohr's oratorio, "Calvary," 1835, where it is set to the words, "If all thy friends forsake thee." This oratorio was translated into English by Edward Taylor, and was first performed at the Norwich Festival in England in 1839. Several other hymn tunes were composed by Spohr, two of which are in the 1887 edition of *Laudes Domini*.

Louis Spohr (he writes it "Louis," not "Ludwig," in his autobiography) was born in Brunswick, April 5, 1784. Both of his parents were musical. His father was a flute player, and his mother was a singer as well as a piano player. He learned the violin, and began to compose at an early age. His first public appearance was at a school entertainment, where he played a concerto of his own composition. In 1805 he obtained a position as leader of the band of the Duke of Gotha, and wrote much of the music that was used by it. In 1817 he went to Frankfort-on-Main, where he became conductor of the opera, later going to London, where he wielded his baton at a Philharmonic concert. He appeared in concerts in many of the large cities of Europe, and his playing was frequently accompanied by his wife, who was an accomplished performer upon the harp. In 1822 Spohr took up his residence at Cassel, where he had accepted a life appointment as chapel master to the elector. While on a leave of absence he was enabled to conduct his oratorio of "Calvary" at the Norwich festival in 1839, but in 1842, when his "Fall of Babylon" was presented at Norwich, the elector refused the necessary leave, to the great disappointment of the composer. He died at Cassel, October 22, 1859.

STOWELL

L. M.

SOLON WILDER

The hymn of Hugh Stowell, "From every stormy wind that blows," is often set to the music of Thomas Hastings, called "Retreat," from a word found in the third line of the first stanza. But this hymn has also been set to music by Solon Wilder, who named his tune from the writer of the hymn. This soprano solo, with quartet accompaniment, is contained in *The Praise of Zion*, a book compiled in 1865 by him jointly with Frederic S. Davenport, and now it is again making its appearance in the hymn books.

Solon Wilder was born December 20, 1830, at Princeton, under the shadow of Mount Wauchuset, the highest point of land in central Massachusetts, and he died in that town forty-three years later, April 6, 1874. He was leader of a choir in Bangor, Maine, for twelve years, and it was while there that his *Praise of Zion* was issued. This book has at least sixty pieces of music with his initial over them. From Bangor he went to Boston, where he spent five years as a teacher in the Conservatory. He conducted musical conventions throughout New England, and in New York, New Jersey, Pennsylvania, Ohio, and Minnesota. His last convention was held in Warren, Massachusetts, only a month before his death. At his funeral two of his compositions, a double chorus, "Rock of Ages" and "Stowell," were sung by sixty members of the Worcester Choral

183

Union, which he had conducted for many years. The following tribute is from a fellow laborer, William F. Sherwin: "He was a Christian man, pure of life, of fine presence and affable manners, with strong personal magnetism and wonderful perseverance. He held high rank as an educator and popularity as a leader."

TALLIS' CANON

L. M.

Thomas Tallis

Thomas Tallis, or Tallys, as he wrote his name, was the father of cathedral music. Quite an extended catalogue of his published music was prepared for Grove's *Dictionary of Music*, and a much longer list of his existing manuscripts, but it is said that there are no secular pieces among them. He devoted his talents entirely to the service of the church. In 1560 *The Whole Psalter* was translated into English verse, presumably by Archbishop Parker. But all doubt as to the authorship of this version was removed when Mr. Lea Wilson, who had a large collection of Bibles and Psalters, discovered that a metrical preface to the 119th Psalm was an acrostic —the initial letters of the sixteen lines spelled MATTHEUS PARKERUS. Following the Psalter are nine tunes by Tallis, two of which have come into common use. The eighth tune is called "Tallis' Canon," or, as somewhat altered in a few hymn books, it is known as "Evening Hymn." A canon is explained as a tune in which, after the air has proceeded for a few notes, another part takes up the same melody, the two running along together, but one part four or five beats ahead of the other. In some alterations of this canon the introduction of slurs has destroyed the canon form. The original was written for an eight-line stanza. Its reduction to a four-line tune fitted it for the evening hymn of

Bishop Ken, "All praise to thee, my God, this night."
The Methodist Hymnals of 1878 and 1905 have used
the first line of this hymn as Thomas Ken wrote it—
"Glory to thee, my God, this night."

TALLIS' ORDINAL

C. M.

The ninth tune at the end of Parker's *Psalter* is
called "Tallis' Ordinal," because it was intended for
use at ordinations. It has no regular setting in
modern hymn books, but is used with various common-meter hymns.

Thomas Tallis is supposed to have been born in
the second decade of the sixteenth century. He died
November 23, 1585, and was buried in the chancel of
the parish church at Greenwich. Both church and
monument have been destroyed, but a copy of his
epitaph was printed in 1720, and from it we quote
two of its four stanzas, in its quaint form:

"Enterred here doth ly a worthy wyght,
    Who for long tyme in musick bore the bell;
His name to shew was THOMAS TALLIS hyght,
    In honest vertuous lyff he dyd excell.

"He maryed was, though children he had none,
    And lyv'd in love full three and thirty yeres;
With loyal spowse, whose name yclept was JONE
    Who here entomb'd, him company now bears."

He was an organist at Waltham Abbey, a position
which he retained until the dissolution of the abbey,
when he received twenty shillings wages and twenty
shillings reward. He then became a Gentleman of the
Royal Chapel. In 1576 he and his pupil, William
Byrd, obtained Letters Patent, giving them the ex-
clusive right of printing music and ruled music

paper for twenty-one years. The first work printed under the patent was his own "Cantiones," a beautiful specimen of early music typography. Tallis also composed a remarkable song of forty parts for eight choirs of five voices each. His pieces show great learning and much dignity, and are calculated to impress by their solemnity and power.

TAPPAN

C. M.

GEORGE KINGSLEY

George Kingsley began to write hymn-tunes as early as 1838, when this tune, "Tappan," was composed, and his music has found a place in a large number of hymn books published since. But the change in taste, or the crowding out of the old tunes to make place for newer ones, has eliminated most of the compositions of Mr. Kingsley from recent books. A number of his tunes were in the Methodist hymn book, 1857; in the *Episcopal Book of Common Praise*, 1867; and in *Songs of the New Life*, 1869, by Darius E. Jones, who was then leading the music in Beecher's Plymouth Church. While Mr. Kingsley was teaching music in Philadelphia, he met Cornelius Everest, and furnished forty-three compositions for his book, *The Sabbath*, issued in 1873. *Laudes Domini*, of Dr. Charles S. Robinson, has fifteen of his tunes, and *The Methodist Hymnal*, 1905, six besides two arrangements of tunes by other writers.

George Kingsley (1811–1884) was a native of Northampton, Massachusetts, and the later years of his life were also spent in that town, in the same house that had sheltered many of his ancestors. Beginning with the *Sunday School Singing Book*, 1832, the number of books which he had compiled had reached ten in 1863. He composed both sacred and secular music, and his series of three volumes of *The Social Choir* has been called one of the best collections of its kind ever made. One has written of his hymns: "Every one of them has melody and spirit. The more I study music, the more I appreciate him." His musical library was given to the Forbes Library of his native town, and in the library museum there is a fine oil portrait of him as a young man.

TELL IT OUT

P. M.

Ira D. Sankey

The missionary hymn of Frances R. Havergal, "Tell it out," has given name to the tune by Ira D. Sankey. His music is very popular for use in Sunday schools, meetings of young people, prayer and social meetings, but the compilers of books for the stated worship of the Sabbath have been slow in admitting the gospel song. Whatever is liked by the people, however, will be sure to gain an entrance into the hymnals, and so this type of song is coming into more frequent use in the regular church service. Tunes of his composition are to be found in three of the seven hymn books named in the preface.

Ira D. Sankey was born August 28, 1840, in the town of Edinburg, Lawrence County, Pennsylvania. His father was a State senator for a number of years. At the age of fifteen the son joined the Methodist Episcopal Church and took up its work as leader of the choir, superintendent of the Sunday school, and he was also president of the Y. M. C. A. He served in the army during the Civil War, and in 1870 he met Mr. Moody, who discovered in him just the man he had been seeking for some years to help him in his work in Chicago. After considering the matter, which meant for him the giving up of his business and the devotion of his abilities to an entirely new venture, he went with the man whose name is invariably joined with his in gospel work. After the Chicago fire in 1871, the two made a tour to England, where their success was immediate. Mr. Moody could not sing a note, could not distinguish one tune from another, but he knew the value of music in his services, and the people were made more responsive to his preaching by the songs of his coworker. The last years of the singer were spent in the night of blindness, but that could not extinguish the light which welled up from within. He died August 13, 1908.

THE NINETY AND NINE

Ira David Sankey

Mr. Sankey (1840–1908) tells us that it was in the year 1874 that the poem, "The Ninety and Nine," was discovered, set to music, and sent on its world-wide mission. He found it one day in the corner of a newspaper, when he was traveling in Scotland, and cut it out thinking it would make a good hymn, whenever he could get a tune for it. Not many days afterward Mr. Moody was preaching about the Good Shepherd, and at the close of his sermon he turned to Mr. Sankey and asked if he did not have a solo that would be appropriate for a closing piece. This poem seemed to be just the one desired, but there was no music for it. "Yet," says Mr. Sankey in telling the story, "I thought I must sing the beautiful and appropriate words that I had found a few days before." So, placing the newspaper slip on the organ before him, he slowly formulated the tune as he sang, and not a note of it has been changed from that day to this. One notices the halting rhythm of the first four lines, moving upon only five tones in nine measures. Then the singer seems to feel sure of his ground, and adds variety to his melody, closing with a strain which is most fitting to the climax of the hymn, "Rejoice, for the Lord brings back his own." The song had not only reached the hearts of his audience, but Mr. Moody had been moved by the words which were so new to him. Mr. Sankey afterward learned that the poem had been written by Elizabeth C. Clephane in 1868, and first published in a magazine, *The Children's Hour*. From thence it was copied into various papers, but little noticed until Mr. Sankey gave it music. Miss Clephane had died five years before this time, and it was in her home town of Melrose that her two surviving sisters heard Mr. Sankey sing the hymn and recognized it as her composition.

TRURO

L. M.

CHARLES BURNEY

The name of Charles Burney is usually associated with this tune, though there does not seem to be conclusive evidence that he composed it. The hymn, "Now to the Lord a noble song," was set to it on its first appearance in *Psalmodia Evangelica: a Collection of Psalms and Hymns for public worship*, by Thomas Williams, 1789. But while that book had a number of pieces to which the name of Burney was attached, this tune was without his name. Doctor Hatfield attributes it to the *Lock Hospital Collection* of 1769, but I have been unable to find the tune in that book, though there are eight other tunes of his in that book.

Charles Burney was baptized under the name of his parents, James and Anna Macburney, but when he grew up he dropped the prefix. He and his twin sister were born April 7, 1726, at Shrewsbury, England, where his father was organist, and the entry of his baptism is made upon the records of the church. He studied music under Thomas A. Arne in London from 1744 to 1747 and was organist in several churches for the next twenty years. He received his degree of Musical Bachelor in 1769 from Oxford. He was one of the most esteemed organists of his time, and besides the church music that he wrote, he composed the music for several dramas. He also prepared a *General History of Music*, a history of

195

Music in Germany, and a *Plan for a Music School.* An essay toward the *History of Comets,* printed in London in 1769, indicates that his studies were not entirely confined to music.   He died at Chelsea, April 12, 1814, at the age of eighty-eight.

URBS BEATA

7, 6

George Fitz Curwood Le Jeune

"Urbs Beata," "The City Beautiful," was composed by George F. Le Jeune in 1887 while he was director of the music at Saint John's Chapel in New York. By the repetition of the first four lines a refrain has been added to the original hymn, which is a very old Latin one. It is frequently used as a processional.

The composer was born in London, England, June 18, 1841. Many books give the year as 1842; the date 1841 was furnished me by his eldest son, who is a prominent organist in New York City. Mr. Le Jeune came to the United States by way of Canada. He began his musical studies in 1863 with the organist of the cathedral at Montreal, later studying harmony and composition with Joseph Barnby. He directed the music in several churches, including the Pearl Street Church in Hartford, Connecticut; Saint Luke's Church in Philadelphia, and the Anthon Memorial Church in New York City. During the centennial year of 1876 he was called to Saint John's Chapel, one of the many chapels of the wealthy Trinity Parish. Besides his regular work in this church he commenced a series of musical services, which became very popular, and his introduction of many of the compositions of the great masters did much to bring them to the attention of the people. He was frequently called upon to give recitals upon the organ in other places. He showed special ability in the training of boys' voices, and his choir of boys at Saint John's was considered one of the best in the country. One of his pupils, G. Edward Stubbs, organist at Saint Agnes, another of the Trinity chapels, has had marked success in this same direction. Mr. Le Jeune died April 11, 1904, in New York City.

VINCENT

8, 4, D.

HORATIO RICHMOND PALMER

This tune is gradually finding its way into the church hymnals. It is in *The Plymouth Hymnal*, Lyman Abbott, 1893, *The Methodist Hymnal*, 1905, and in the last named year it was placed in the hymnal of the Christian Church, *In Excelsis*, under the name "Scoville." Each time it is used with the hymn "Just for to-day." This hymn has an interesting history because for a long time its author was unknown. It was ascribed to E. R. Wilberforce in several hymn books, and this error is still perpetuated in very recent books. It is of Roman Catholic origin, a nun, Sybil F. Partridge, of Liverpool, England, having written it. The publishers of that church have issued it as a leaflet, but the hymn as used in Protestant books is somewhat altered by the omission of some stanzas that are better suited to Catholic doctrine.

Horatio R. Palmer was born April 26, 1834, at Sherburne, New York. He was educated at Rushford Academy, and in Europe. He began his choral work soon after the close of the Civil War, even then being the organist and director of a choir in western Pennsylvania. The extent of such work is indicated by the fact that for seven years he was in charge of the Church Choral Union of New York, and for fourteen years he directed the Summer Music School at Chautauqua, New York. He has composed many tunes that have come into common use, "Peace, be still," and "Come, sinner, come," while perhaps his best known piece is, "Yield not to temptation." He has written a *Piano Primer*, and a *Biographical Dictionary of Musicians*. Outside the field of music he has lectured on astronomy, the Holy Land and the Orient. He died in November, 1907, at Yonkers, New York.

WATCHWORD

6, 5, D.

HENRY SMART

The tune written for Henry Alford's hymn, "Forward be our Watchword," and first used in the *Church Hymnary*, 1872, is there called "Smart." Many editors, who have copied it into American books, have given it the name "Watchword," and in a few it is called "Forward."

Henry Smart (1813–1879) was one of the popular writers of hymn-tunes in the nineteenth century. Organists have varied experiences in their work, and Smart was no exception. He was an intimate friend of Best, and dedicated one of his choral works to him. An unfortunate printer's error made his inscription to the first edition read: "To his fiend, W. T. Best." Another story which illustrates his facility in transposition is given by Lightwood. He once played "Miles Lane" in the usual key of B flat; between the first and second verses his interlude was modulated very cleverly and almost imperceptibly into the key of B, one semitone higher. Between the second and third verses the key became changed to C, when it was found that the high notes on "Crown Him" did not come out with their former facility; between verses three and four the pitch was again raised another semitone, and so on, until the high notes must have joined the company of the "Lost Chord." He edited two tune books, a *Presbyterian Hymnal* for use in Scotland, and for which he wrote twenty tunes, and a *Choral Book* for the use of the congregation of Saint Luke's. He contributed to the second edition of *Hymns Ancient and Modern,* and twenty-three of his tunes are in the *Church Hymnary,* 1872.

WELLESLEY

8, 7

Lizzie S. Tourjée Estabrook

"Wellesley" is not such a well-known tune except among the Methodists. That denomination used it soon after its composition in its hymnal of 1878, of which Miss Tourjée's father was one of the musical editors. Whether this was its first appearance in print I cannot say, but I have found no earlier use of it. It is also in *The Methodist Hymnal* of 1905, and *The Methodist Sunday School Hymnal,* 1911. The *Hymnal of Praise,* 1913, compiled by Edward Dwight Eaton and William Henry Sallmon for use in colleges, also has it. The composer was a member of the Newton (Mass.) high school when she was asked to set the graduation hymn to music. It was probably thought that because she was the daughter of Dr. Eben Tourjée, founder and director of the New England Conservatory of Music in Boston, she must have abilities like her father, but tune writing was a new idea for her and she shrank from the attempt. Her father, however, encouraged her, and, putting before her the words of the hymn which it was to fit, the tune was evolved, which Doctor Tourjée named for the new college near by. The *Tribute of Praise* was a very popular hymnal during the seventies, edited by Doctor Tourjée, and copyrighted as early as 1871. Later editions were prepared for various denominations, and in a special edition for the Conservatory of Music, 1884, this

tune was introduced.   It had been inserted in the
Methodist book in 1878 over the hymn, "Mighty God,
while angels bless thee," and on the same page with
Faber's hymn, "There's a wideness in God's mercy."
It is now generally used with the latter hymn.

Lizzie S. Tourjée was born in 1858, and after
securing her musical education she became a teacher
of piano in her father's school.   August 16, 1883,
she married Franklin Estabrook.

WOODSTOCK

C. M.

DEODATUS DUTTON, JR.

In 1830 Deodatus Dutton, Jr., and Elam Ives, Jr., published *The American Psalmody*, a collection of sacred music, comprising a great variety of psalm and hymn-tunes, set pieces, anthems, and chants, arranged with a figured bass for the organ or pianoforte, to which is prefixed a new system of teaching musical elocution, or the art of singing. "Woodstock" was one of the tunes composed by Mr. Dutton, and it was set to the hymn of Mrs. Phebe H. Brown, "I love to steal awhile away." Nathaniel D. Gould, in his *History of Church Music in America,* says that this hymn and tune will be associated with Mr. Dutton's "name, and handed down to future ages, and sung by many on earth, while he is singing the Song of Moses and the Lamb in heaven." The name is from the town of Woodstock in Connecticut.

Deodatus Dutton was born in 1808 in Monson, Massachusetts, a town which by a coincidence was the home of Mrs. Brown during the later years of her life. Her hymn had been printed in the Village Hymns of Asahel Nettleton in 1824, and he had suggested the tunes called "Darby" and "Plymouth," but in recent hymn books wherever the hymn is used the tune of Dutton is placed with it. He was a graduate in 1828 from Washington College, now Trinity, in Hartford, and was the poet of his class, reading a poem called "Hartford." He was chosen to play the first organ in Center Church in Hartford in 1822, when only fourteen years old. He was pursuing his preparation for the ministry in the city of New York, and had been licensed to preach by the Third Presbytery of that city when he died December 16, 1832. He was buried from one of the Dutch Reformed churches.

WOODWORTH

L. M.

William B. Bradbury

"Woodworth" made its first appearance in the *Mendelssohn Collection*, 1849, also called Hastings' and Bradbury's *Third Book of Psalmody*. There it is set to a hymn by Elizabeth Scott, "The God of love will sure indulge." As late as 1871, when it was used in the *Tribute of Praise*, it is set to these same words. But in recent years it has become intimately associated with the hymn of Charlotte Elliott, "Just as I am, without one plea." It is found with this hymn in five of the books mentioned in the preface, the Unitarian book, only, omitting both hymn and tune.

Two dates, 1816–1868, will give the period during which William Bachelder Bradbury lived. From the age of twenty-five until his early death his name was one of the most familiar in musical circles, whether in the secular school, the Sunday school, or the services of the church. His first compilation was *The Young Choir, or School Singing Book*, issued in 1841 with Charles W. Sanders, whose series of spellers and readers were in common use in the schools. This book had one hundred and forty-four pages, and contained sixteen pieces contributed by Mr. Bradbury. Collections of various types of music followed each other rapidly, until fifty-nine books had appeared with his name on their title pages. Another side of Mr. Bradbury's work was his connection with the early history of the piano-forte. In 1848 F. C. Lighte had entered the field of piano manufacture in New York, and five years later Bradbury joined the firm. In 1861 the Bradbury piano came into being, and was a very popular instrument for many years. His connection, however, was of only short duration, as he withdrew in 1867, and his death followed the next year.

WORSHIP

L. M.

KARL P. HARRINGTON

"Worship" is one of thirteen tunes contributed by Karl P. Harrington to *The Methodist Hymnal* of 1905, and so far as I know it is not found in any other book. Professor Harrington was one of the musical editors, and that fact will account for the number of new tunes from his pen that find a place there. It is set to the hymn of Richard Watson Gilder, "To Thee, Eternal Soul, be praise," which also made its first appearance in *The Methodist Hymnal*.

Karl Pomeroy Harrington was the son of Calvin Sears Harrington, one of the members of the committee for the revision of the *Hymnal* of 1878. He was born June 13, 1861, at Great Falls, New Hampshire, graduated from Wesleyan in 1882, taking his Master's degree three years later. Teaching has been his business ever since, beginning in the high school in Westfield, and continuing in Wesleyan Academy in Wilbraham. He was professor of the Latin language and literature from 1891 in the University of North Carolina, the University of Maine, and Wesleyan University at Middletown, Connecticut, the latter from 1905. During all of his career he has been actively engaged in musical work. While extending his studies in Germany he was organist and choirmaster in the American Church in Berlin. While in Maine he played organs

209

in Bangor and in Orono. In like manner he served
churches in North Carolina and in Connecticut. He
has also conducted a number of musical organiza-
tions. As an author he has written or assisted in
the preparation of a number of books relating to
classical studies, and has edited several books of
music. Besides *The Methodist Hymnal*, already referred to, may be mentioned *The Wesleyan Song
Book* and *Songs of All the Colleges.*

ZION

8, 7, 4

THOMAS HASTINGS

"Zion" is found as early as 1831 in *Spiritual Songs for Social Worship*, compiled by Lowell Mason and Thomas Hastings. It is there set to the hymn of Thomas Kelly which bewails the fact that Zion was long in hostile hands; but the sacred herald brings the message that "Great deliverance Zion's king will surely send." The tune is still used in many books with this hymn.

Thomas Hastings was several years older than Lowell Mason, but they worked together on the book of 1831, just quoted, which became very popular and reached seven editions. This was not, however, the first book that Doctor Hastings had compiled. In 1816 a small collection had been prepared by him, which later was combined with another arranged by Solomon Warriner of Springfield, Massachusetts, and the two appeared under the name *Musica Sacra, or the Utica and Springfield Collection*. For twenty years this was in common use, and ten editions of it were printed. Thomas Hastings was a writer of hymns as well as a composer of music. Six hundred hymns may be placed to his credit, and over three hundred tunes and other pieces of music. He began his musical career as the leader of the village choir in the small pioneer community of Clinton, New York. He then undertook the organization of singing schools, which from that time occupied much of

his attention.   After a few years' residence in Utica,
New York, where his books were published by William Williams, one of the earliest printers in that
State, he moved to New York City, which thenceforth
was his home until the date of his death.

BIOGRAPHICAL CALENDAR

JANUARY

3, 1830. b. Alexander Ewing
6, 1806. b. George Hews
7, 1868. d. W. B. Bradbury
8, 1792. b. Lowell Mason
13, 1731. bapt. John Darwall
22, 1748. b. Lewis Edson
22, 1876. d. John B. Dykes
23, 1858. d. John Wyeth

FEBRUARY

3, 1832. b. W. H. Doane
10, 1783. d. James Nares
10, 1819. b. Richard S. Willis
16, 1886. d. C. S. Harrington
18, 1546. d. Martin Luther
26, 1773. d. Thomas A. Arne
26, 1846. b. G. C. Stebbins

MARCH

4, 1875, d, John E. Gould
10, 1823. b. John B. Dykes
12, 1872. d. Conrad Kocher
14, 1826. b. W. F. Sherwin
14, 1884. d. George Kingsley
15, 1770. b. William Gardiner
26, 1827. d. L. v. Beethoven
31, 1732. b. F. J. Haydn
31, 1770. b. John Wyeth

APRIL

3, 1836. b. R. M. McIntosh
5, 1784. b. Louis Spohr
6, 1874. d. Solon Wilder
7, 1726. b. Charles Burney
11, 1904. d. G. F. C. LeJeune
12, 1716. b. Felice Giardini
12, 1814. d. Charles Burney
14, 1886. d. W. F. Sherwin
16, 1829. d. C. G. Glaser
19, 1715. bapt. James Nares
26, 1834. b. H. R. Palmer

MAY

1, 1858. d. George Coles
4, 1784. b. C. G. Glaser
7, 1900. d. Richard S. Willis
10, 1770. d. Charles Avison
13, 1842. b. A. S. Sullivan
16, 1850. b. Arthur H. Mann
17, 1826. b. C. S. Harrington
20, 1884. d. Silas J. Vail
22, 1781. d. Earl of Mornington
31, 1809. d. F. J. Haydn

JUNE

1, 1798. b. S. B. Marsh
2, 1792. b. George Coles
5, 1752. b. George Burder
13, 1861. b. Karl P. Harrington
18, 1841. b. G. F. C. LeJeune
28, 1712. b. J. J. Rousseau

JULY

2, 1778. d. J. J. Rousseau
2, 1916. d. A. H. Messiter
4, 1873. d. George Hews
6, 1899. d. R. M. McIntosh
6, 1879. d. Henry Smart
7, 1811. b. George Kingsley
11, 1895. d. Alexander Ewing
14, 1875. d. S. B. Marsh
17, 1895. d. M. M. Wells
19, 1735. b. Earl of Mornington
21, 1831. b. T. E. Perkins
31, 1846. d. Peter Ritter

AUGUST

3, 1820. b. L. O. Emerson
11, 1872. d. Lowell Mason
12, 1885. d. H. K. Oliver
12. 1912. d, W. G. Fischer

AUGUST—Continued

13, 1908. d. Ira D. Sankey
14, 1727. d. William Croft
14, 1810. b. Samuel S. Wesley
14, 1824. d. Hugh Wilson
17, 1828. b. G. W. Warren
28, 1840. b. Ira D. Sankey
29, 1763. buried. J. Chetham

SEPTEMBER

 4, 1844. d. Oliver Holden
10, 1858. d. H. W. Greatorex
18, 1765. b. Oliver Holden
20, 1795. b. Charles Zeuner
28, 1903. d. Samuel A. Ward
29, 1915. d. L. O. Emerson

OCTOBER

 2, 1815. b. M. M. Wells
 4, 1743. d. Henry Carey
 6, 1816. b. W. B. Bradbury
 6, 1818. b. Silas J. Vail
 7, 1783. d. William Tans'ur
14, 1835. b. W. G. Fischer
22, 1859. d. Louis Spohr
23, 1819. b. I. B. Woodbury

OCTOBER—Continued

26, 1813. b. Henry Smart
26, 1858. d. I. B. Woodbury

NOVEMBER

 7, 1857. d. Charles Zeuner
10, 1483. b. Martin Luther
16, 1853. d. William Gardiner
22, 1900. d. A. S. Sullivan
23, 1585. d. Thomas Tallis
24, 1800. b. Henry K. Oliver

DECEMBER

 2, 1764. bapt. Hugh Wilson
10, 1815. b. John Zundel
16, 1772. b. L. v. Beethoven
16, 1786. b. Conrad Kocher
16, 1796. d. Felice Giardini
16, 1832. d. Deodatus Dutton
20, 1830. b. Solon Wilder
24, 1813. b. H. W. Greatorex
24, 1915. d. William H. Doane
26, 1836. d. Hans G. Naegali
28, 1848. b. Samuel A. Ward
28, 1870. d. Alexis F. Lvoff
30, 1678. bapt. William Croft

INDICES

INDEX OF FIRST LINES OF HYMNS

INDEX OF WRITERS OF HYMNS

INDEX OF COMPOSERS

INDEX TO THE TUNES